C000260492

Self-esteem

The costs and causes of low self-worth

Nicholas Emler

The **Joseph Rowntree Foundation** has supported this project as part of its programme of research and innovative development projects, which it hopes will be of value to policy makers and practitioners. The facts presented and views expressed in this report are, however, those of the author and not necessarily those of the Foundation.

© Joseph Rowntree Foundation 2001

All rights reserved.

Published for the Joseph Rowntree Foundation by YPS

ISBN 1 84263 020 2

Prepared and printed by:
York Publishing Services Ltd
64 Hallfield Road
Layerthorpe
York YO31 7ZQ
Tel: 01904 430033; Fax: 01904 430868; E-mail: orders@yps.ymn.co.uk

Contents

Acknowledgements

The following have offered helpful advice on different parts of this review: Dominic Abrams, University of Kent; Roy Baumeister, Case Western Reserve University; John Bynner, Institute of Education; William Damon, Stanford University; Duncan Cramer, Loughborough University; Leon Feinstein, the London School of Economics; Miles Hewstone, University of Wales at Cardiff; Peter Robinson, Bristol University; Glen Waller, St George's Hospital Medical School.

1 Self-esteem: definition and measurement

Introduction

Violent children hold other lives cheap because they believe their own lives to be worthless.

(Melanie Phillips, *The Sunday Times*, 3 December 2000, commenting on the apparently motiveless murder of a young Nigerian boy, Damilola Taylor)

This observation will have struck a chord with readers because it mirrors many widely accepted views. These include the ideas that many children, rather too many, are now growing up with a sense that they have no value, and that their damaged sense of their own worth in turn causes them to do violence to themselves and others. If such views have a sound basis in fact, then there is much to recommend efforts to repair the self-esteem of these young people and to take whatever measures we can to ensure no further damage of this kind is done. Are these views therefore well founded?

The aim of this review is to summarise what is known from research about the nature of self-esteem, its consequences and its antecedents. More particularly, it is concerned with the self-esteem of children and adolescents. The reasons for this focus are twofold. First, many of the phenomena seen to be consequences of low self-esteem are especially pronounced in the early part of life. The once popular image of adolescence as a 'stormy decade', a period of life marked by chronic self-doubt, conflict with parents and rebellion against the standards of adult society, has proved to be an unhelpful and inaccurate generalisation about young people. A recent study confirms this point. Gillies *et al.* (2001) interviewed ordinary young people and their parents and found little to suggest that their relationships with one another were riven with disputes and difficulties.

There is, however, less dissent from the observation that adolescents are, much more than other age groups, liable to commit crimes, abuse drugs and put their health at risk in other ways. And, of course, some matters of concern are by definition associated with this period of life, such as teenage pregnancy. The second reason for a focus upon adolescence is the sense that damage done and left unrepaired early in life cannot thereafter easily be undone.

There is an incidental and not entirely trivial advantage to defining the scope of the review in this way: most of the published literature deals with this period of life. The real disadvantage is that little can be selected out as having no relevance for the aims of the review. Nonetheless, we can and should be more precise about the aims and scope. The issues of interest here are essentially whether individuals differ in self-esteem, whether these differences have any important consequences and, if so, what produces these differences.

The review will be organised as follows. Following a brief overview of popular views about self-esteem, scientific interpretations of the concept will be described. This will lead into an examination of the options for measuring self-esteem, and whether there are grounds for regarding it as a unitary quality and as one distinct from some apparently related psychological attributes. Next will come a review of evidence for behavioural consequences of low self-esteem; particular attention will be given to those consequences seen to constitute social problems, such as delinquency, drug abuse, teenage pregnancy, racism and suicide attempts. Research into the roots of self-esteem will then be considered, aiming in particular to determine what is known about the conditions resulting in low self-esteem. Finally, methods of intervention are considered: what kinds of intervention appear to be successful in raising self-esteem, what are their costs and what evidence is there if any that they have long-term benefits?

Self-esteem in the public domain

If there were ever a magic bullet that could transform a young person's life it would be a pill coated with self-esteem. This powerful yet fragile quality is the key to the future for a teenager.
(Katz, 2000, p. 7)

Few ideas in the human sciences have ever achieved the level of attention that has been lavished upon the notion of self-esteem. Within psychology alone, research papers and articles that make some reference to self-esteem, and often much more than a passing reference, are now appearing at a rate of over a thousand each year. Given this level of interest, one is liable to conclude that it is an idea of some considerable significance. But, rather more unusually, this academic preoccupation is substantially matched by interest among the public at large, and not just among those people – doctors, teachers, social workers – who might be expected to show a professional interest in the human psyche. In their everyday lives, people routinely treat the notion of self-esteem as an intelligible basis for explaining their own difficulties or others' failings. Some indication of the sheer level of this popular interest is that the US bookseller Amazon currently lists over 2,000 titles which deal in some way with self-esteem.

In a sense, the prominence of this notion in everyday discourse should cause no surprise. The term is not the property of psychology or indeed any other branch of the human sciences; nor did it begin life as a psychological concept with a specialised and technical meaning. This particular composite term has been in common usage in the English language, according to the *OED*, for at least four centuries. And, when a term endures for so long, it is a reasonable bet that it refers to something of importance to people, something they find it very useful to be able to label for one another.

Nevertheless, over time, usage changes and the connotations evolve. It is in this respect that scientific interest in self-esteem is related to the public discourse. When we talk about self-esteem in our everyday conversations, somewhere in the background – and not always only in the background – a psychological interpretation is being invoked. Self-esteem is about psychological health, about motivations, about personal identity. Perhaps the most striking and distinctive feature of contemporary usage, however, is the idea that self-esteem is a kind of resource or asset. And, like other assets, it is now discussed within the realm of human rights. People desire self-esteem, just as they may be expected to desire prosperity, good physical health, or freedom of thought. But they also regard it as something they should have by right. And, if they lack self-esteem, this is because they have been denied or deprived of it through the actions or inactions of others.

The human sciences have made this aspiration legitimate, even admirable, in an interesting way. They have encouraged the belief that self-esteem is good for the individual who is blessed with it but it is also good for society. In other words, this is a case in which self-interests coincide with the common good. And this puts it firmly on the political agenda. If self-esteem is good for collective well-being, it is worth spending public money to ensure there is more of it to go around. This is a far from fanciful scenario. In 1986, the state of California set up a task force to achieve precisely this aim. Its remit was to raise the self-esteem of its entire population.

Why did politicians in California back this initiative? The reasoning is instructive; more than that, it reflects directly on the purpose of this review. The Californian policy makers had come to be convinced that self-esteem is a powerful, all-purpose 'social vaccine' – the term used in the Task Force final report (California Task Force to Promote Self-esteem and Personal and Social Responsibility,

1990). It had become a fashionable notion that high self-esteem inoculates people, and in particular young people, against vulnerability to a wide range of social ills. Those who possess high self-esteem are less likely to abuse drugs, commit crimes, fail to benefit from education, engage in unsafe sexual practices that could pose a risk to health or result in unwanted pregnancies, suffer from stress, develop eating disorders, perpetrate acts of racism or child abuse or violence towards their partners, become chronically dependent on the state for financial support, get depressed or make suicide attempts. And the list of benefits didn't stop there.

Farmers have been told that high self-esteem will contribute more to their success than up-to-date knowledge of farming methods. Bankers have been advised to nurture the self-esteem of their customers because this will significantly contribute to the latter's net worth; customers with high self-esteem will be more likely to repay loans and provide profitable business to the bank. Even management consultants have sought to convince their clients that staff with good self-esteem will be more effective and productive employees (Hewitt, 1998).

Self-esteem has therefore proved fertile territory for those Hewitt (1998) describes as conceptual entrepreneurs. These are people who seek to persuade a wider audience that something is a major problem and it requires a solution; they also claim to know what the solution is. In this case, their claims that low self-esteem lay behind a range of undesirable behaviours and practices made low self-esteem the problem and high self-esteem, or methods that supposedly promote this condition, the solution. In Californians, they had a receptive audience for these claims but also, it turned out, across the world (see foreword in Mecca *et al.*, 1989).

Correspondingly, the fashion favoured associated forms of political correctness. Because self-esteem is both desirable for society as a whole and the right of every individual, all practices or circumstances that could conceivably damage a person's self-esteem were to be purged from the curriculum of life (and certainly from the precincts of educational establishments). Any reluctance to pursue this agenda could be attacked with all the self-righteous moral certainty of a lynching party. Thus, as one commentator noted, around the time of the California initiative, teachers and others working with young people became increasingly reluctant to voice meaningful relative judgements about those in their care (Baumeister, 1998). Announcing winners meant others were losers. Genuine criticism was far too risky. Consequently, standards got dumbed down and every ego required a merit award just for turning up.

The note of scepticism here is intentional, the intention to signal what is to come in this review. Like the fictional Gordon Gekko's infamous admonition about greed, we should be suspicious of any convenient convergence of self-serving interests with the greater good.

What has become common sense in this matter – only people with low self-esteem act in ways that are harmful to themselves or others – turns out as a blanket generalisation not to be a reliable or sound basis for policy initiatives.

If we are to spend money – anybody's money – or time or talent on efforts to mitigate social problems, we had better be sure of two things: those efforts will have the anticipated benefits and investments made in them would not have been better spent on something else. Of course, one cannot always be entirely sure ahead of time of either of these things. It may simply be impossible to tell without at least a trial effort whether something will work, let alone whether it will be cost-effective. But, in the case of self-esteem, we can make highly educated guesses. And we can make them if we are prepared to be educated by the effort already lavished upon the pertinent issues by social researchers across the globe.

What is self-esteem? The views of scholars and scientists

In common usage, self-esteem is a favourable opinion of oneself. Psychologists, however, from the very start addressed the underlying question raised by such an appraisal: on what is it based? The most likely answer it now seems, rather surprisingly, is 'not much'. But this possibility has only recently come into focus.

Most discussions of the question pay some homage to the definition offered by William James in his *Principles of Psychology*, first published in 1890: self-esteem is success divided by pretensions. The elegant simplicity of this notion contains some interesting implications. Self-esteem can be increased by achieving greater successes and maintained by avoiding failures, but it can also be increased by adopting less ambitious goals: 'to give up pretensions is as blessed a relief as to get them gratified' (James, 1890, p. 311). James's formula also made the important prediction that self-esteem cannot be predicted purely from the objective level of success a person achieves. What matters is whether their successes are relevant to their aspirations. Thus, to the detached observer, particular individuals may indisputably be highly successful, to the extent of being widely admired for their achievements, and yet these same individuals may have a very negative opinion of themselves because these achievements are either irrelevant to their pretensions or fall short of them. And, as we shall see later, James also expected individuals to differ in their average levels of self-esteem.

The consequences of James's formula come down to the following question: is there in practice more variance in the denominator or in the numerator? If most people aspire to achieve the same things – which is to say there is little variance among people in their pretensions – then the main cause of differences in self-esteem would be differences in degree of success, and we should expect these two things to be strongly related. On the other hand, if there is a great deal of variance in pretensions – people differ considerably in *what* they aspire to and/or in the standards they aspire to – objective differences in success become less important sources of differences in self-esteem.

There is evidence that young people, whatever their circumstances, want or aspire to much the same things, at least in a material sense. So, for example, young people from deprived areas share conventional aspirations for their adult lives – 'nice house, good job, nice car, nice family' (Johnston *et al.*, 2000). But self-esteem is more closely linked to aspirations for personal qualities, and here aspirations are more variable. Thus, Rosenberg (1979) found that not all adolescents cared equally about being likeable. In contrast, concern with appearance is, according to Harter (1993), just about universal.

The success/pretensions formula also clearly implies a calculation or judgement and therefore raises further questions about the basis on which this calculation is made. Most obviously, how do people know whether and to what degree they are successful, that they have the qualities they desire? A highly influential answer to this question was given by the sociologist Charles Horton Cooley in 1902. Our assessments of our own worth are based on the judgements we imagine *others* make of us. Moreover, our guesses about these judgements depend upon the qualities we see in these other people. We anticipate that virtuous or successful people will judge us more harshly than people who lack these attributes. In other words, what shapes our self-esteem are not our objective accomplishments objectively and directly appraised, but the anticipated judgements of these accomplishments by other people. And, when these other people are themselves very successful, our own successes will look less impressive.

These ideas were to reappear much later in three guises that have been relevant to scientific thinking about self-esteem. First of all, Leon Festinger (1954) developed his social psychological theory of social comparison processes. Its essence is the idea that we seldom have access to objective and absolute standards against which we can judge ourselves. There are some obvious respects in which this is true. We may, for example, wish to have good taste in music or sensible opinions about the issues of the day. But there is no objective test we can apply to ourselves here as we can, for example, to the question of whether we are able to swim 50 yards or stay upright on a bicycle. Even with respect to such matters of performance, however, as often as not we want to know whether we are *good* at swimming, cycling, etc., and not merely whether we can do these things. And, in order to estimate how well we are doing, we need to compare ourselves with others – to make social comparisons. So, it is crucial *who* we choose for comparison. Much of the research following on Festinger's propositions sought to determine how such choices are made.

Second, Morris Rosenberg (1965) devised a method for measuring self-esteem based on the notion that it is a variety of attitude. Attitude had emerged as a key concept in the social sciences almost 40 years earlier; this had coincided with the development of procedures for measuring social attitudes with some degree of precision. Once social attitudes could be measured, the effects upon behaviour of differences in attitudes could be studied. Attitudes were defined primarily in terms of emotional or evaluative reactions; they constitute our reactions of approval or disapproval, liking or dislike, for social practices, habits of behaviour, categories of people, political policies, public figures and so on. And it was in this sense that Rosenberg regarded self-esteem as an evaluative attitude towards the self. A great merit of this view is that it corresponds quite closely to common usage or the dictionary definition of self-esteem. The link to Cooley was Rosenberg's belief that this

attitude is powerfully shaped by what others are believed to think of the self. The enduring significance of Rosenberg's definition is that it is embodied in his self-esteem scale and this scale has become the gold standard in self-esteem research.

The third long-term impact of Cooley's ideas has been the sociological tradition of symbolic interactionism and its notions that we discover who we are and what we are through our interactions with other people and through the access these interactions give us to their opinions of us. Most of the research into and theorising about self-esteem has assumed that we are strongly affected by others' reactions to us. If the feedback we receive from other people is uniformly negative, this will be absorbed into our self-appraisals. If other people overwhelmingly react with approval then our self-esteem will inevitably benefit. It is also an assumption behind just about every intervention programme yet devised to raise self-esteem as well as the basic premise of most of the popular books devoted to raising self-esteem. One such example, *501 Ways to Boost your Child's Self Esteem* (Ramsey, 1994), is simply a list of different ways and opportunities for giving positive feedback to one's children. Finally, the same assumption lies behind views about criticism: one should never give negative feedback because its effect violates the other's inalienable right to self-esteem.

Cooley, it should be recalled, emphasised in particular what we *imagine* others think of us: 'We imagine, and in imagining share, the judgments of the other mind' (p. 152). We should remember this emphasis because it is possibly quite crucial to understanding the nature and roots of self-esteem. It might seem a reasonable step from this observation to the conclusion that what we imagine to be the case has a basis in our experience. In other words, our suppositions about what other people think of us are derived from how they actually treat us. Nonetheless, these two things are not necessarily the same. As we shall see when the determinants of self-esteem are discussed later in this review, however reasonable it may be in theory to make the link, research supports a very different conclusion.

Let us return for the moment to the nature of self-esteem. Opinions, we assume, differ. If self-esteem is one's opinion of oneself, how might the self-esteem of one person differ from that of the next? William James thought that self-esteem would vary in two ways. First, it would behave rather like an emotion; it would fluctuate, if not from hour to hour then certainly from day to day and perhaps from week to week. One person might experience higher self-esteem than another one week but their positions could be reversed the following week. This view takes self-esteem to be reactive, the reactions being to the variable or changeable conditions of a person's daily life. So, just as an insult might provoke anger or unexpected difficulties with some project might induce a mood of gloom, warm praise or a significant success could temporarily elevate self-esteem while a humiliating failure might have the opposite effect.

If self-esteem does vary in this way, then there are two relevant questions for us. First, how reactive is self-esteem? Can it, for example, be lowered or raised very rapidly and does it recover to some resting state rather slowly – is self-esteem more analogous to grief (a relatively long-term reaction from which one recovers slowly) or to fear (relatively short-term)? Second, do individuals differ in the reactivity of their self-esteem? Do some people respond to every minor change in fortune with a rapid adjustment to their opinion of themselves while others are very slow to react and difficult to shift? Some recent research does suggest that differences of this kind exist and that they may have important consequences, but primarily in combination with more stable or chronic differences in self-esteem levels.

A related notion is that self-esteem is akin to a barometer in that it tracks conditions rather than reacting to events. For one advocate of this view, Mark Leary, the relevant conditions are the state of one's relations with others (e.g. Leary *et al.*, 1995). When these relations are good – when one is accepted, included, loved – then self-esteem will be relatively high. When relations are bad – when one is rejected, excluded, despised – then self-esteem will be low. For Leary, the significance of this tracking is that it initiates, or should initiate, corrective action when things are not going well. In other words, low self-esteem acts as a warning about the poor state of one's relationships with other people and a signal that repair work is needed.

If Leary is right, then two things potentially follow. One is that the particular judgements others make of our successes, assets and talents are ultimately of less consequence for our self-esteem than whether they like and accept us. The other is that self-esteem itself may be of less consequence than the quality of the personal bonds with others that it reflects.

The barometer notion is close to the idea that self-esteem is a motivator. People experience a need for self-esteem: when they have less of it they will strive to obtain more. But this does not preclude the possibility that this need will be more strongly felt by some than by others, just as some people are more concerned than others to achieve success or might experience more keenly than others a need to be liked and accepted. In other words, the desire and search for self-esteem could be a more potent driving force in the lives of some individuals than they are in the lives of others. Thus far, there seems to be little evidence for this. Everyone seems to prefer self-esteem and to find the lack of it distressing (e.g. Brown, 1993). But not everybody finds it so easy to achieve and hold on to.

This brings us closer to the second way in which William James anticipated self-esteem might vary.

He thought that each person carries 'a certain average tone of self-feeling' and this average will vary from one individual to another. This is similar to what would be called in contemporary psychology a 'trait' view of self-esteem – it is a quality of the person that is relatively fixed or persistent. The crucial word here of course is 'relatively'. Just how fixed are the differences? Are they like adult stature, pretty much permanently fixed once people are full-grown, or more like weight differences – modifiable within limits but gradually and with difficulty?

The conclusions one comes to about these questions have implications for how one tries to measure self-esteem as well as for the consequences that might be expected to flow from variations in self-esteem. Most of the research to be examined in this review has treated – and measured – self-esteem as a trait rather than as a state, and has asked about the consequences of chronically high versus chronically low self-esteem. At the same time, however, many researchers, and certainly the conceptual entrepreneurs, have taken the view that chronic low self-esteem can be raised (and correspondingly that high self-esteem can be eroded; it can suffer long-term damage). In this, their implicit if not explicit model of self-esteem is close to Rosenberg's: it is an attitude. If the attitude is well established and strongly held, it will resist change, it will be stable but it will not be entirely immune to modification. If it is not strongly held, it will be more unstable, more likely to go up or down with changing circumstances and more readily modified by interventions that have this particular purpose.

The truth or otherwise of views about the changeability of self-esteem is of considerable practical importance. But their truth should in the end be determined on the basis of evidence and not assumed a priori. Some of the relevant evidence is provided by the process of building and testing methods for measuring self-esteem, and it is to measurement that I now turn.

Can self-esteem be measured and, if so, how?

Research can tell us nothing about self-esteem, and certainly nothing about either its causes or its consequences, if self-esteem cannot first be measured. A procedure or instrument to perform this task of measurement must be able, at the very least, to do two things. First, it must be able to detect differences or changes in self-esteem. Ideally, it should be sensitive to differences or changes that are quite small. Second, it should not be sensitive to changes or variations in other psychological states or qualities. These two requirements may be obvious enough but achieving them both in practice has been far from easy.

In designing a method of measurement, it also helps to be clear about what it is one wishes to measure. In the case of self-esteem, as we have seen, clarity on this point – or at least unanimity – has been missing. The requirements for measuring a motive are not identical to those for measuring an attitude and for both they are quite different from what is required to assess a temporary state. Most of the procedures developed have followed Rosenberg's lead and taken self-esteem to be an attitude.

Nonetheless, this still leaves a lot of choice about how to measure self-esteem. The main choice is whether to treat attitudes primarily as feelings, or as evaluations. Coopersmith defined self-esteem as 'the extent to which a person believes himself to be capable, significant, successful and worthy'. This definition therefore stresses *evaluation* – a set of judgements about the self against criteria of excellence.

In contrast, Rosenberg's (1965) scale, which was one of the first and is still one of the most widely used measures of self-esteem, emphasises *feelings*. One attraction of his scale is its simplicity. The basic scale consists of just ten statements of opinion about oneself and one is simply asked whether one agrees with the sentiment expressed or not (see the box below). A score is the sum of positive views expressed out of ten.[1]

The Rosenberg Self-esteem Scale (RSE)

1 On the whole I am satisfied with myself.

2 At times I think I am no good at all.

3 I think that I have a number of good qualities.

4 I am able to do things as well as most other people.

5 I feel I do not have much to be proud of.

6 I certainly feel useless at times.

7 I feel that I am a person of worth, at least on an equal plane with others.

8 I wish I could have more respect for myself.

9 All in all, I am inclined to feel that I am a failure.

10 I take a positive attitude towards myself.

There are two distinctive features of the scale. The first is that agreement with any of these statements is not agreeing that one is better than or superior to others. Indeed, only two of the ten statements make any reference to a comparison with other people and in each case the sentiment expressed is one of parity with others. The second is that the sentiments are very general evaluations of oneself. For this reason, it has appropriately been described as a measure of global self-esteem.

A merit of this assessment strategy is that this simple scale achieves quite a high level of precision. Any measurement procedure is subject to some error; in practice, this means that attempts to measure the same quality several times will on each occasion produce a different result. Small differences can be tolerated; large differences would be a serious problem. Fortunately, there are now well-established procedures for improving the

precision of psychological measures and, just as important, for quantifying the degree of precision one has achieved. But, because high degrees of precision in measurement are costly, there will always be a trade-off between the conflicting goals of reducing error and keeping measurement costs down.

The low cost and relatively low error of the Rosenberg Self-esteem Scale have therefore made it very attractive for researchers. Nonetheless, different instruments are useful for different purposes, for example to achieve a finer level of discrimination than a ten-item scale allows – to detect very small differences – or to assess particular elements of self-esteem.

According to one review (Blaskovich and Tomaka, 1991), at least 200 different measures of self-esteem have been developed; there can be few other concepts in the social sciences, apart perhaps from intelligence, of which this is true. This is potentially a serious problem; merely because different tests or scales are claimed to measure the same thing, it does not mean that they do. Fortunately, the problem is simplified for us a little. Just four scales have accounted for the majority of published studies, the RSE (described above), the Coopersmith (1967) Self Esteem Inventory (SEI), the Tennessee Self Concept Scale (Fitts, 1965) and the Piers-Harris Children's Self Concept Scale (Piers, 1969). Thus, for most purposes, we need only know whether these four measure the same quality.

Rosenberg's measure was originally devised to study adolescents and is regularly used with adults as well. Younger children require a different approach. Stanley Coopersmith (1967) was particularly interested in the self-esteem of preadolescents, specifically ten to 12 year olds, and to study this developed a 50-item inventory (SEI). But Coopersmith also took the view that self-esteem is most appropriately assessed by measuring distinct components. This view directly reflects his definition of self-esteem which, as noted above, emphasises evaluation rather than feeling. Consequently, his inventory includes questions about self-esteem in four areas of the child's life: parents, peers, school and personal interests.

The SEI has been described as an aggregate rather than a global measure because self-esteem is treated as the sum or aggregate of assets and liabilities in various domains – in this case, the four areas of life that Coopersmith took to be most relevant. Given that correlations between the SEI and Rosenberg's measure are not especially high – in the range 0.58 to 0.60 (Blaskovich and Tomaka, 1991) – these two instruments are not measuring precisely the same thing, even after taking measurement error into account. The other two extensively used scales, the Tennessee Self Concept Scale and the Piers-Harris Children's Self Concept Scale, are also aggregate measures. Overall, scores derived from the various aggregate measures tend to correlate well with each other; typical ranges are 0.65 to 0.85 and this higher value is approaching the theoretical limit, which indicates that they are pretty much assessing the same thing.

The choice of instrument for research is therefore going to depend on the following considerations:

- appropriateness to the sample studied (children and adolescents require different approaches)

- the value of being able to assess particular facets of self-esteem; for example, versions of one instrument include scales for social confidence, physical appearance, school abilities and physical competence in addition to general self-regard (Fleming and Courtney, 1984)

- the importance of being able to compare results with published norms (in almost all cases, the published norms are based on American samples and are not necessarily appropriate to other populations)

- costs (also short scales may also be more acceptable to some research populations, particularly if they are being asked many other questions).

There are, however, some other measurement issues we need to consider. Knowing that one has measured something with a reasonable degree of precision is not the same as knowing *what* one has measured or whether it is what one intended to measure. This is familiar in psychometrics as the issue of validity. Any instrument serving as a thermometer should be sensitive to changes in temperature but not to changes in anything else such as air pressure. Likewise, an instrument to assess self-esteem should be sensitive to variations in this quality but not to variations in any other.

The validity of a measure is commonly decided by looking at three patterns of evidence. First, do different methods of measuring the same phenomenon produce similar results? Second, are these results quite distinct from those obtained by using similar methods to measure what are presumed to be quite different phenomena? Third, do test scores behave in a manner that is consistent with what is known or believed to be the nature of the phenomenon?

All the commonly used methods for measuring self-esteem rely upon people's self-reports of their feelings or opinions of themselves. Only two alternatives have so far seriously been considered. One is to use observers to assess a person's self-esteem. Observer ratings are widely used in personality research and generally the results converge with those from self-reports. This is regarded as important evidence of validity because it indicates that results are not primarily reflecting the method of measurement used.

Matters, however, have so far proved quite different for self-esteem. Demo (1985) assessed the self-esteem of adolescents both in the usual manner, using the Rosenberg and Coopersmith scales, and using ratings by their peers and by student observers. The two self-report measures were interrelated as were the two observer rating measures, but the self-reports were largely unrelated to the observer ratings.

It is not quite clear what we should make of this. But one possibility is that the observers were assessing something different; rather than judging how these other individuals actually felt about themselves the observers may have been estimating how they ought to feel about themselves, perhaps on the basis of their other apparent qualities. Given that, as we shall see, how people feel about themselves bears little relation to their objective qualities or accomplishments, there would then also be little agreement between self-evaluations and evaluations by observers.

The second alternative to self-reports is the use of indirect measures. These rely on unconsciously and automatically activated mental connections and have already been used with apparent success to measure other kinds of attitudes. Farnham *et al.* (1999) have applied the same principles to develop an implicit measure of self-esteem. Unfortunately, they found virtually a zero relation between this measure and the most widely used self-report measure, the RSE. Their own interpretation is that it is the *latter* that is the poor measure of self-esteem. Before we accept their conclusion, however, we should consider the other two tests of validity.

The first of these is that instruments intended to measure self-esteem should not produce the same results as instruments intended to measure other qualities. Up to a point, self-esteem measures have little difficulty in satisfying this test. What they are measuring is clearly distinct from what is measured by instruments intended to assess qualities such as extraversion or conscientiousness, for example. The difficulties arise with respect to qualities that appear on the surface to be more similar to self-esteem.

One of the most conspicuous examples is depression. Measures respectively of self-esteem and depression consistently produce similar results; individuals who score highly on self-esteem measures typically have low scores on measures of depression and vice versa. This raises questions as to whether depression and low self-esteem are not the same thing. It also casts some doubt on the coherence of trying to explain one in terms of the other. On the other hand, it has been argued (e.g. Tennen and Affleck, 1993) that depression as a clinical state – a condition serious enough to merit medical care – is qualitatively distinct from low self-esteem. Perhaps the most reasonable conclusion for the present is that, when research measures degrees of depression in samples that are not undergoing treatment for this condition, it probably is measuring an attribute that substantially overlaps with low self-esteem.

Measures of self-esteem also tend to produce results similar to measures of such qualities as locus of control (the degree to which individuals believe they control events in their lives), self-efficacy (the degree to which individuals believe they possess the capabilities necessary to achieve things and control events) and neuroticism (the degree to which individuals describe themselves as insecure, fearful, guilt-ridden and miserable). At least one researcher, Judge (2001), believes these similar results reflect the fact that these all show the same underlying quality, which he calls core self-evaluations.

If Judge is right, this is helpful in two respects. First, we can avoid wasting time over questions as to whether self-esteem or a quality labelled in one of these other ways is the more important influence on some outcome, such as, for example, suicide attempts or eating disorders. Second, it expands the knowledge base available to us. Thus, for instance, evidence about the nature, causes or consequences of neuroticism is potentially informative about the nature, causes or consequences of low self-esteem.

The third test of validity is whether measures of self-esteem produce results that make sense. In effect this is asking: are the results consistent with the theories we have about this quality? So-called test–

retest correlations – whether the same results are obtained if self-esteem is measured at two closely related points in time – provide reassurance that self-esteem is, as Rosenberg and others proposed, a relatively stable quality of the person. Or, as William James put it, each individual has a 'certain average tone of self feeling'. But James also seems to have been right in his view that an individual's self-esteem can fluctuate from day to day around this average level. In other words, self-esteem is a state as well as a trait (Hetherton and Polivy, 1991).

As the points in time at which self-esteem is measured become further apart, the results obtained on these separate occasions also become less similar. What this indicates is that self-esteem has moderate but by no means perfect stability over time. People's self-esteem can change as they grow older even if there is a tendency for it to become progressively more stable with age.

Stability itself, however, turns out to be a variable quality (Kernis, 1993). Some people have high or low self-esteem that is also very stable, at least over short periods (a few days). Others show much more instability in their opinions of themselves over the same periods. This is consistent with Rosenberg's view that self-esteem is an attitude. We should expect attitudes to vary in strength. When they are strongly held they will be more stable. When they are held with less certainty they will be more vulnerable to contradiction and so liable to fluctuate as each new piece of evidence comes along. We should therefore expect stable self-esteem to be more resistant to efforts to change it. It also turns out, as we shall see, that stability of self-esteem has consequences for behaviour.

As to the rest, it comes down to the following question: does the picture provided by the research evidence as a whole – which will include evidence about the causes and consequences of self-esteem – make sense? If it does, then there are grounds for confidence that the measures that have contributed to this picture do detect real and consequential differences between people.

Conclusions

Low self-esteem is the source of all manner of personal and social ills. That at least is the popular view. Whether systematic research can either confirm or qualify this popular opinion requires first the availability of procedures – tests or measures – that can accurately assess levels of self-esteem. And this in turn depends on a degree of clarity as to what it is one is trying to measure. There has been broad agreement that self-esteem can usefully be regarded as a form of attitude and measures constructed on this assumption have been able to meet a basic test; they are able to assess the level of *something* with a fair degree of reliability or precision. Currently, the major point of disagreement about this something is whether it is best regarded as a generally positive or negative feeling about the self or as a collection of judgements about personal assets and liabilities.

Whether this attitude is a feeling or a set of judgements, it also has the properties of both a state and a trait. It can vary from day to day but it also has an average level that is relatively stable over time. So, some individuals may have a particularly positive opinion of themselves that changes little over the years, even if it may vary somewhat around this generally high level from one day to the next.

The measures of self-esteem currently available to researchers can also to some extent meet the important test of divergent validity; they are sensitive to variations in this quality rather than some others. The question mark that remains, however, is whether variations in self-esteem are really something distinct from opinions about the self that go by such labels as depression, neuroticism, self-efficacy and locus of control.

Finally, these measures all rely upon self-reports. It is good practice in psychological measurement to demonstrate that one can obtain similar results using different methods of measurement. With respect to self-esteem, this has yet to be demonstrated. But this should not discourage us from looking for patterns of evidence with the methods of measurement that are available. And, if those patterns are coherent and consistent, this should increase our confidence in the validity of these methods.

2 The consequences of self-esteem

The problem of distinguishing causes and effects

Self-esteem crosses over from a topic of purely theoretical interest to one of real practical importance to the extent that it has consequences, and more precisely consequences having benefits and costs. Indeed, this conviction, that there are extensive and in particular negative consequences of low self-esteem, has fed wider public interest in the matter. The legions of 'conceptual entrepreneurs' referred to previously have survived and multiplied on the back of this certainty. So, is it a sound and sensible appreciation of what matters in life?

To answer this we need to recognise two distinct kinds of consequence. Probably the more familiar one is that variations in self-esteem influence the occurrence of some outcome of interest, for example whether or not a person makes repeated suicide attempts, becomes an alcoholic or physically abuses their own children. In other words, the issue here is: do differences in self-esteem make these negative outcomes more or less likely?

The second consequence is for the effect of other circumstances or conditions on such outcomes. This kind of consequence is sometimes referred to as a buffering effect (typically used to describe the effects of high self-esteem in reducing the impact of adverse life events on such outcomes as mental or physical health). However, buffering is one of a set of effects under the general heading of 'moderators' (cf. Baron and Kenny, 1986). Moderator effects are potentially at least as important in practical terms as are causal effects, but we tend to know much less about them, probably because they are less easy to spot.

Still the most commonly adopted option in research is to look for a correlation between self-esteem and the other variables of interest. An example of this is the study by Robinson and Frank (1994) comparing the self-esteem and sexual behaviour of a sample of young people. Suppose these researchers had found no association between self-esteem and pregnancy in adolescence – which is pretty much what they did find. It might seem reasonable to conclude that self-esteem has no consequences in this area. But this inference would be an error.

Of the two major types of error that arise from interpreting data, the more common – the 'Type II' error – is to accept the null hypothesis when it is in fact false. If this is labouring an elementary point it is still a point we should not take for granted; establishing conclusively that two things – such as low self-esteem and teenage pregnancy – are entirely *unrelated* is extremely difficult and for practical purposes virtually impossible. Consequently, a high proportion of the conclusions that social scientists are able to draw from their work are tentative and provisional. In this case, the reasonable and appropriate conclusion that Robinson and Frank draw from their findings, and for us to draw, is that there may be an association and there may not but the data available do not say which of these is true. As to what would allow a choice between these two possibilities, the answer essentially is that more data would. And quite possibly only rather a lot more data.

So much for the downside of null effects (or failures to reject the null hypothesis). The good news is that for many of the questions likely to be of interest to us a lot more data probably are available. But their availability also changes the questions we now can and should ask. This is because most things *are* related, or to continue with the example, there is almost certainly a relation between a woman's self-esteem and whether or not she has a pregnancy as a teenager. So, what we really need to ask is not whether there is a link or not but how strong is the link.

Though most things are related, many of the relationships are very weak indeed, so weak as to be of virtually no practical significance. This may be the reality of any self-esteem–teenage pregnancy link. We can in principle provide this more precise and useful answer by systematically combining the evidence from all the available and relevant studies. This puts us in a position to capitalise on the considerable number of studies of self-esteem and its possible consequences. The techniques involved here are those of 'meta-analysis' (Rosenthal, 1994) and because they can answer this more precise question – just how strong is the link? – they are set to become increasingly important tools for social scientists and policy makers, and indeed for everyone interested in the practical applications of scientific evidence. Later, I will look at the application of this technique to the link between self-esteem and gender, and consider the further question that must then arise: how strong must the association be to have any practical significance?

For the moment, however, consider in the simple case what a positive effect – a rejection of the null hypothesis – means. Too often it is taken to be an answer. In reality, it merely raises a question: why does the relationship exist? To see why, we need only recall what all science students are told in their first year: an empirical association between two observations – a correlation – in itself tells us nothing about the causal relationships that link these observations. If, for example, we discover that delinquent teenagers have lower self-esteem than their more law-abiding peers, it does not follow that low self-esteem leads to delinquency, or for that matter that delinquency lowers self-esteem.

There are basically seven possibilities we need to consider. It is important to distinguish between these possibilities because each has distinct practical implications, though it might not be immediately apparent why this is so. Let us, therefore, consider in turn the different ways in which self-esteem could be related to behaviour or other outcomes.

1   *It is a direct contributory cause that is independent of other causes.* This might involve the demonstration, for example, that level of self-esteem has an impact on risk taking in sexual behaviour (e.g. unsafe sexual practices carrying a higher risk of sexually transmitted disease or unwanted pregnancy) independent of or over and above the effects of other factors predictive of such risk taking. The two practical implications are that (a) one might thereby reduce the level of risk taking by increasing self-esteem and (b) one might identify groups – i.e. those with low self-esteem – most vulnerable to the outcome of interest and concentrate resources upon them to reduce the impact of *other* risk factors.

2   *It is a mediator.* This means that self-esteem is the psychological state that links some cause to an effect. Let us suppose, for example, that teenage girls who do poorly in school are at greater risk of becoming pregnant. Self-esteem would mediate this effect if academic failure damaged self-esteem and if this diminished esteem then increased the likelihood of pregnancy in the teenage years. The practical value of this lies in the possibility that at least one link in the causal chain can be broken, most obviously that between academic failure and feelings of self-worth. Should this prove possible then the experience of failure need not increase the risk of pregnancy.

3   *It is an indirect or mediated cause.* Low self-esteem could, for example, affect the likelihood of teenage pregnancy indirectly through its impact on susceptibility to peer influence. The causal chain could then be broken at the mediator.

4   *It is a moderator.* This is not necessarily the same as saying that self-esteem interacts with other causes, even if in practice most moderator effects so far discovered take this form. Let us suppose that a connection has been found between poor educational performance and teenage pregnancy. Self-esteem would be having a moderating effect if this connection were present or stronger at one level of self-esteem (e.g. low) and absent or weaker at another level (e.g. high). This has two kinds of practical implication. One arises from the possibility of modifying self-esteem. If it could be raised, then the impact of the cause on the effect would be diminished. The other is the potential to identify an at-risk group.

5   *It is a correlated outcome.* Suppose that experience of early teenage pregnancy is associated with low self-esteem. It is possible that both low self-esteem and pregnancy are consequences of something else such as intercourse with multiple partners or poor relations with parents. If this is the case then the association between pregnancy and self-esteem is merely incidental.

6   *It is an effect.* A different possibility is that pregnancy as a consequence of early sexual activity itself damages self-esteem. In effect, pregnancy becomes the mediator of a link between such activity and self-esteem. There are practical implications if the causal repercussions then lead on from lowered self-esteem to other negative outcomes (such as depression, suicide attempts, drug abuse, or prostitution). Obviously, we are going to be most interested in the causes of self-esteem if we think low self-esteem has damaging consequences.

7   *It is both cause and effect.* Some of the theoretically derived predictions about self-esteem anticipate that level of self-esteem will affect the likelihood of certain actions or behaviours and that the occurrence of these latter will in turn have effects on subsequent levels of self-esteem. But in some cases the causal loop is expected to involve negative feedback. For example, suppose low self-esteem increases the risk of teenage pregnancy which in its turn, if it occurs, *raises* self-esteem (this possibility has been taken seriously – see section on 'Risky sexual behaviour' later in this chapter; it has also been taken seriously for another outcome, delinquency – see section on 'Crime and delinquency' later in this chapter). In other cases, there is supposedly a positive feedback loop – for example, between self-esteem and the formation of close relationships. On closer inspection, however, it almost always turns out that additional links are in the loop and that the loop is not perfectly closed. Practically, this means that causal loops can be broken.

In practice, almost all of the research that has examined possible effects of self-esteem on such outcomes as health-threatening behaviour patterns, anti-social activities, poor life management (poor work habits, etc.) has been conducted in such a way that it cannot distinguish between direct or indirect causal influences, mediators, correlated outcomes or effects. In particular, wherever a relationship has been found between self-esteem and some pattern of behaviour, it has not been possible to rule out these last two possibilities – either that some other condition affects both self-esteem and the behaviour in question or that this behaviour influences self-esteem.

Research that can distinguish between the various possibilities therefore assumes particular value in deciding policy implications. Two research designs are especially important here. The first is a longitudinal design (or prospective study) in which self-esteem and/or an outcome are, at the very least, measured on more than one occasion. In the case of a link between teenage pregnancy and low self-esteem, for example, one would want to know whether low esteem predated the pregnancy. Prospective studies in which psychological states at one point in life can be compared to events later in life can in principle answer such questions. But, a large initial sample may be required if the events of interest – such as suicide attempts or addiction to Class A drugs – have a low incidence in the population studied. Moreover, if self-esteem does change over time, then a real impact of low self-esteem upon suicide attempts at 13, 14 or 15, or drug addiction in the late teens and twenties may not be detected if self-esteem has been assessed at, for instance, age ten. In evaluating evidence from longitudinal studies, therefore, one needs to consider the time interval between successive observations or measurements.

The second research design of interest is a true experiment. Its high status in scientific research is quite simply a consequence of its unique power in deciding questions of cause and effect. But it is still not a perfect solution for such questions. If we were able to lower the self-esteem of one group of people and could then show that, compared to another group which had not suffered this experience, members of this first group were for example more willing to commit misdemeanours, we could be fairly confident that this behaviour was caused by their lowered self-esteem. But it would not follow that, beyond the conditions of this experiment, low self-esteem is a cause, let alone the main cause, of criminal misconduct. This stronger conclusion, that the results of the experiment have general or external validity, requires something additional. It requires proof that the conditions that allowed us to lower self-esteem in the experiment also occur naturally and with the same effect.

This point is not always recognised by those scientists who are the most enthusiastic about the value of experimental evidence. Yet the point is particularly relevant with respect to self-esteem. It becomes clearer if one asks whether a person whose self-esteem has just been lowered is really equivalent to one whose self-esteem has been low for a long time. It is a fair guess that these are two very different kinds of people who could respond to the same circumstances – such as the opportunity to commit some misdemeanour – in quite different ways. One simply cannot reproduce, in the course of an experiment, effects that in the normal course of events have accumulated over a lifetime (De Ronde and Swann, 1993, p. 157 make a similar point).

Despite this difficulty in generalising from experimental findings, the potential value of experiments should not be discounted. There are many cases of researchers trying to raise self-esteem as part of some programme of intervention or treatment for a particular group. The group might be victims of rape or child abuse, patients with eating disorders or alcohol addiction, or young offenders. These cases provide valuable opportunities to test a causal hypothesis. If the intervention does succeed in raising the self-esteem of a treatment group, as compared to that of a control group, is there also a change in the relevant behaviour? More specifically, is degree of change in self-esteem directly related to the scale of any change in behaviour? This would be important evidence of a causal role of self-esteem in that behaviour. Sadly, this opportunity has not always been taken.

Matters of consequence

Diminished self-esteem stands as a powerful independent *variable (condition, cause, factor) in the genesis of major social problems.* We all know this to be true.
(Smelser, 1989, p. 8, first emphasis in original, second emphasis added)

This statement appears in the introduction to a collection of scientific reviews commissioned by the California Task Force on self-esteem. What makes the statement extraordinary is the observation Smelser adds next: 'The real problem is … how can we determine that it is scientifically true.' The implication is that the role of science is to confirm what we already know to be the case. This is not an auspicious beginning for a book that is intended to be a dispassionate, objective survey of scientific evidence. But it does make the conclusions in the final report of the Task Force, published one year later (California Task Force to Promote Self-esteem and Personal and Social Responsibility, 1990), less surprising.

The authors of that report present as key findings essentially what 'we all know' to be true. In the end, any evidence that pointed in a different direction – including evidence reviewed in the 1989 volume – was not allowed to get in the way of this certainty. Before taking our own look at the evidence, what constitutes 'a major social problem'?

Smelser proposed that it must first be relevant to something we value as a society. 'Pregnancy out of wedlock, for example, is a problem in large part because it stands in violation of the value we place on the family as the legitimate locus for childbearing' (Smelser, 1989, p. 3). With respect to teenage pregnancy in particular, one might argue it is additionally a problem because of the value we place on childhood; teenage pregnancy threatens to bring childhood to a premature end.

The behaviour should also involve some economic or social cost. Prevalence is one but not the only determinant of the scale of such costs. The economic costs of common crimes – burglary, assault, car theft – are high not least because of the treatment meted out to convicted offenders. Ironically, however, the costs for victims are far lower than those of corporate crime though this latter kind of crime is seldom identified as a social problem.

The behaviour also needs to be sufficiently commonplace. Killing people with handguns was not, in this sense, a social problem in Britain even before the post-Dunblane ban on these weapons. It might be regarded as such in the United States where deaths from gunshot wounds are many times more prevalent (though the powerful gun lobby there has effectively kept it off the social problem agenda). In contrast, politicians, journalists and others in both countries routinely identify teenage pregnancy as a major social problem on grounds of its high prevalence rate.

Behaviour qualifies as a social problem, therefore, if it is defined as such at the political level. Behaviours that objectively meet other criteria are not invariably treated by governments as social problems while others that fail to meet them are. As sociologists like Howard Becker have made clear, what gets to be treated as a major social problem, and its relative position on the scale of society's priorities, is strongly determined by the activities of moral entrepreneurs. Child labour is accorded the status of social problem in some countries while in others it is regarded as an integral and essential part of the economy. Amphetamine abuse is not conspicuously identified as a social problem in Britain but marijuana use supposedly is such a problem.

The point of these observations is to acknowledge that no listing of behaviours under the banner of social problems will be uncontroversial. Nor can it claim to be entirely objective. To review the role of self-esteem in the genesis of social problems, the best that one can do is to consider behaviours that do have clear and significant costs and about which there is enough research to allow some sensible conclusions. This latter requirement will exclude quite a lot that one might otherwise wish to consider.

With these caveats in mind, the following list is proposed:

- crime and delinquency (and violent crime)

- racial prejudice

- abuse of illegal drugs (and tobacco use)

- alcohol abuse

- risky sexual behaviour (including practices carrying risk of sexually transmitted diseases and of teenage pregnancy)

- child maltreatment

- educational underachievement

- chronic dependency on state support

- eating disorders

- suicide and suicide attempts/parasuicide.

Crime and delinquency

Including crime, and juvenile crime in particular, on a list of costly social problems will cause little dissent. It is worth saying, however, that the catalogue of costs should include those to the lives of the offenders and not just those for victims or those for the state in terms of prevention, policing and treatment.

There have been three serious arguments for the role of diminished self-esteem in criminal behaviour. First, there are versions of the argument in the opening quotation from Melanie Phillips. People who are convinced they are worthless have

no self-esteem to lose from any opprobrium they might attract by breaking the law. The flip side of this is the assumption that people with high self-esteem avoid crime because they anticipate that it would damage their sense of their own worth.

The second argument puts together two beliefs about young people and crime. One is that young people are drawn into crime to the extent that they succumb to the malign influence of less law-abiding youngsters. The other is that young people with a low sense of their own worth are more susceptible to influence of this kind.

The third argument has been called by its principal advocate, Howard Kaplan (1980), an 'esteem enhancement' explanation for crime. This explanation takes self-esteem to be a motive: children want to think well of themselves, find it distressing when they do not and therefore make efforts to enhance their esteem if it is low. According to this explanation, delinquency (Kaplan uses the term 'deviance') follows on low self-esteem because it provides a means of raising esteem.

The first two arguments predict a straightforward association between low self-esteem and delinquent behaviour. Kaplan's interpretation gives rise to a more complex set of predictions: low self-esteem should produce an increase in delinquent behaviour which should in turn result in higher self-esteem. That is, level of self-esteem should be both cause and effect. How these various predictions fare against the evidence[1] is provided in the Appendix.

The final report of the California Task Force (California Task Force to Promote Self-esteem and Personal and Social Responsibility, 1990) is unequivocal. 'People who esteem themselves are less likely to engage in ... crime' (p. 5). However, their own academic consultants, Scheff *et al.* (1989), find the opposite message in the same evidence: 'the conclusion we draw from the reviews, [that] the relationships reported between self-esteem and deviance have been weak or null' (p. 177).

McCarthy and Hoge (1984) are equally unequivocal:

We find ... no clear positive policy implications in the weak results of our analysis ... if researchers cannot uncover stronger relationships between self-esteem and delinquency than we have, they should look in other directions in order to understand both self-esteem and delinquency.

So far, none has found stronger relationships. There are indications of a slight effect of involvement in delinquency upon subsequent self-esteem, but the effect is to depress self-esteem slightly, not to raise it (see Appendix, section on 'Crime and delinquency'). None of the other predictions made by Kaplan and others has been borne out; in particular no study to date has shown that low self-esteem leads to delinquency.

Violent crime

Violations to self-esteem through insult, humiliation or coercion ... are probably the most important sources of anger and aggressive drive in humans.
(Feshbach, 1971, p. 285)

Even if there is no link from self-esteem to delinquency, could matters be different for violent crime? Feshbach was by no means the first to suggest a link. An old idea in psychology had it that aggression was usually a response to some frustrating experience; crudely, if your efforts to achieve something you want badly are frustrated you are liable to lash out (Dollard *et al.*, 1939).

In the 1960s, this kind of response to frustration was explicitly linked to self-esteem. According to Rosenbaum and de Charms (1962), persons with low self-esteem are more easily frustrated and hence more prone to aggression. Quite how they reached this conclusion is unclear given their further assumption that low self-esteem is associated with lower expectations. If you expect less, surely you should be less often disappointed or 'frustrated'.

Nonetheless, the conviction that high self-esteem must necessarily be a good thing – an opinion one encounters again and again in this literature – favoured the Rosenbaum and de Charms view. For example, re-examination of evidence collected from a sample of young men in the 1930s led its authors to the conclusion that boys who were consistently aggressive had become so because sustained parental attacks had undermined 'the boy's conception of himself as a person of worth and significance' (McCord *et al.*, 1961, p. 84).

A famous and frequently cited study of prison inmates with a history of violence reached a similar conclusion. Its author, Hans Toch (1993), proposed that their violent behaviour was most often 'self-image compensating', intended to repair a damaged self-image. Or, as Scheff *et al.* (1989) put it, 'the need to resort to aggression was believed to stem from feelings of extremely low self-esteem' (p. 170).

Similar claims have been made about other forms of violent behaviour including rape, domestic violence, child abuse, gang violence and murder. Against these claims, the negative evidence in the case of delinquency points to the same conclusion, if only because violence is an integral feature of this pattern of behaviour (Emler and Reicher, 1995). And this is the conclusion that others have come to.

A careful review of the claims that low self-esteem leads to various forms of violence (Baumeister *et al.*, 1996) makes two points that are worth repeating here. One is that there is little research directly testing this causal link. In other words, researchers have often invoked low self-esteem as an explanation for violence without actually measuring self-esteem adequately if at all.

Their second observation is that insofar as sound evidence is available it does not support the view that chronically low self-esteem leads to violence. It is, on the contrary, more consistent with the view that violence results from a *high* level of self-esteem. Baumeister and his colleagues go on to qualify their own prediction in an important way. It seems that high self-esteem carries with it a greater risk that this very positive view of the self will be contradicted or challenged by others. It is this challenge that precipitates violence. This is also a plausible reading of Feshbach's opinion, in the quotation above: your self-esteem is more likely to be violated the more of it you have in the first place.

For the moment, it is worth noting that the authors of another study (Kernis *et al.*, 1989) found that the people most likely to report angry and hostile responses to others had high but unstable self-esteem. Those with high and stable self-esteem were the least likely to report such reactions. This seems to confirm the value of recognising that self-esteem can vary in stability and not just in chronic level. It is also an example of self-esteem acting as a moderator and doing so in such a way that no simple association with the outcome would be evident.

Racial prejudice

What we are trying to tackle in this one hour is what I think is the root of all the problems in the world – lack of self-esteem is what causes war because people who really love themselves don't go out and try to fight other people.

(Oprah Winfrey, cited in Harrison, 1989)

Racism is now high on the agenda of most western countries as a significant social problem. This is partly because equality of rights irrespective of ethnic background is recognised and enshrined in law. Discrimination based on race has long ceased to be official policy in most countries. Its persistence, along with other forms of intolerance, such as homophobia, has thus become a social problem seen to be rooted in individual attitudes. It is undoubtedly also on the agenda because so

many of the armed and most deadly conflicts of recent times appear to have had their origins in animosities based on ethnicity or race.

There have been various arguments for a link between self-esteem and racial prejudice. The most extensively developed and thoroughly researched theoretical explanation for such a link is social identity theory. A difficulty in deciding whether the evidence supports this explanation, however, is that there is some disagreement as to exactly what it predicts.

The essence of this explanation, as originally set out by Henri Tajfel (1978), seems to be as follows. Individuals are members of social groups or categories and derive a part of their sense of who they are – their identity – from membership of these categories. The worth or status of the groups to which they belong also reflects on their sense of their own personal worth. In other terms, social identities are potentially sources of self-esteem.

However, the worth or standing of the groups to which we belong can only be determined relatively, by comparing them with other groups to which we do not belong. To the extent that we wish to think well of ourselves, we are therefore bound to look for ways in which our own group is better than another. But we will also do what we can to promote and protect this superiority. Among other things, we should therefore show favouritism towards our own group and discriminate against others whenever the opportunity arises.

Some of this prediction has certainly been borne out by research. People do show an 'ingroup bias' in all manner of ways. They will tend to regard their own group as more virtuous in comparison with others and they will discriminate in favour of their own group when possible. However, the crucial claim is that this favouritism is motivated by and satisfies a desire for self-esteem.

One prediction to which this analysis gives rise is the following: if people are not able to discriminate their self-esteem should suffer; if they are able to do so their self-esteem should benefit. Of

12 attempts to test this prediction identified by Rubin and Hewstone (1998), nine were able to confirm it. A further proposal is that the tendency to discriminate in favour of one's own group and against others will be most marked in those individuals with the strongest need to increase their self-esteem, namely those who initially have least. This particular prediction has received little support. Instead, most experimental tests of this prediction – 22 out of 23 – showed that discrimination was highest amongst those whose self-esteem was initially highest (Rubin and Hewstone, 1998). Another review of the available evidence (Aberson *et al.*, 2000) came to the same conclusion: more ingroup bias is actually shown by people with high, not low, self-esteem (cf. also Crocker and Schwartz, 1985).

There is now a debate among those working in this area of social psychology as to whether the kind of self-esteem that may be a factor in ingroup favouritism is social or collective self-esteem rather than personal, specific rather than global, or state rather than trait (Brown, 2000). It remains to be seen whether the resolution of these questions will shed any more light on the determinants of racism. However, one other issue yet to be resolved satisfactorily is the relation between the effects found, both in laboratory experiments and outside, which involve fairly modest degrees of favouritism for an ingroup and the often extreme degrees of violent hostility sometimes shown towards members of ethnic minorities.

A different approach treats racial prejudice as an attitude that varies from one individual to another. There are good grounds for this approach: some people are consistently more inclined to endorse racist sentiments than others – and indeed this tendency is associated with other kinds of bigotry, including sexist and homophobic attitudes (e.g. Altemeyer, 1996). The association between racist attitudes and limited formal education is also very clear (Emler and Frazer, 1999). It might therefore be expected that racist attitudes go together with low self-esteem. However, this link has not been found; indeed, if anything, the link appears to be between racism and *high* self-esteem. The assumption that poor educational attainment necessarily lowers self-esteem may therefore be at fault. I shall consider this possibility in Chapter 3.

Abuse of illegal drugs

> ... *drug addicts behave as they do because of low self-esteem, rather than developing low self-esteem as the result of deviant behaviour.*
> (Kitano, 1989, p. 319)

Low self-esteem has been one of the most popular explanations for drug abuse, according to Furnham and Lowick (1984). But just what kind of an explanation is it? The two clearest grounds for expecting a causal link between self-esteem and drug abuse treat the latter as respectively criminally or morally deviant behaviour and as a health risk.

From the observation that use of certain drugs is illegal and may be labelled as morally deviant by mainstream society follows the expectation that people will use or abuse these drugs if they already have a poor opinion of themselves; if in effect they have nothing further to lose from public condemnation or criticism. This is essentially the same as one of the arguments for a link between delinquency more generally and low self-esteem.

Second, taking seriously the idea that self-esteem is one's attitude towards oneself, if that attitude is negative then it should involve treating the self badly. Drug abuse would represent bad treatment if the abuser were knowingly incurring a significant health risk.

A third explanation attributes drug use to peer influence. This attribution is quite explicit in the 'just say "no" to drugs' type of campaign directed at youth. It also routinely supplies a justification for intervention programmes targeted at drug use where these programmes include attempts to raise self-esteem (e.g. Coombs *et al.*, 1984; Franklin, 1985). The reasoning here, as with delinquency, is that low self-esteem renders adolescents vulnerable to undesirable peer influences.

A fourth possibility is that drug use, insofar as it makes the user feel good, offers to people whose self-esteem is low a means of raising their esteem or of at least a temporary escape from the bad feelings they have about themselves. But this possibility highlights a problem, as do some of the others: drug *use* and drug *abuse* are not equivalent. Nor is there a simple dividing line between the two, let alone a simple definition of abuse (or misuse or problem use). Yet, despite these difficulties, there are strong indications that the determinants respectively of use and abuse/problem use are not identical (e.g. Glanz and Pickens, 1992; Lloyd, 1998).

Each of the four explanations outlined above assumes that low self-esteem enhances the risk of illegal drug use, if not drug abuse. The evidence for either kind of link is mixed at best. At worst, it suffers from the familiar problems of correlational research: it is not possible to tell whether low self-esteem has a causal influence.

As matters stand, research evidence provides little or no support for the view quoted at the beginning of this section (see Appendix, section on 'Drug use and drug abuse'). If self-esteem is related to drug use, the relationship is weak at best. Furthermore, there is even less to indicate that low self-esteem is a cause, direct or otherwise, of drug use, or of drug abuse. Evidence that draws a clearer distinction between use and abuse might revise these conclusions but McCarthy and Hoge's (1984) recommendation concerning delinquency seems equally appropriate here. There are many, more plausible candidates for the causal roles in both use and abuse of illegal drugs.

Smoking

Studies assessing the link between self-esteem and drug use have quite frequently also considered

tobacco use. Yet there are grounds for treating these activities differently. Unlike illegal drug use, the illegality of buying and smoking cigarettes is purely a function of age. Moreover, public attitudes to smoking and smokers are rather different from those towards illegal drugs and those who use them. The current focus of these attitudes, and indeed of public campaigns against smoking and of regulations aimed at smoking, is on damage to health. The newer twist is that the health concerns are now extended to people exposed to others' smoking, and this has given a moral dimension to criticisms of smokers.

Smoking is therefore increasingly treated as an anti-social activity and this stigma may have an impact on the self-esteem of those who smoke. But smoking by young people is still widely seen as driven by peer group pressures. Thus, smoking by young people, like illegal drug use, has been attributed to their inability to resist these pressures. And the same assumptions can be found linking susceptibility to peer group pressure with low self-esteem. The personal health risks of smoking are also increasingly salient. This again raises the expectation that people who do not value themselves will do less to take care of their health.

In the light of this expectation, a substantial study of adults – in this case 3,000 navy personnel – by Abood and Conway (1988) produced surprising results. Self-esteem did not predict specific activities liable to affect health, such as smoking, though it did predict what they called the general practice of 'wellness' behaviours. The clear predictor of specific health-related activities was the degree of value each individual attached to his or her health.

With respect to children and adolescents, there does not yet appear to be a case for a strong causal influence of low self-esteem with respect to taking up smoking (see Appendix, section on 'Smoking'). Certainly, there is little at this time to justify efforts to raise the self-esteem of young people if the expected pay-off for such efforts is that they will either give up smoking or not take it up in the first place. This is also the conclusion reached by Dielman *et al.* (1984) on the basis of a study of about 500 12 to 13 year olds. The link found between self-esteem and smoking in this sample was too weak, they thought, to make a case for intervention focusing on self-esteem.

Alcohol abuse

If ... the adolescent lacks self-esteem, behaviors dangerous to health are more likely to occur. These include precocious and unprotected sexual behavior; the use of tobacco, alcohol and other drugs; injuries arising accidentally from risk taking behaviors, especially when combined with alcohol or drugs; intentional injury whether self-inflicted or inflicted by others.
(Friedman, 1989, p. 309)

The social mores surrounding alcohol consumption are different again from those applied to either illicit drug use or smoking. Alcohol consumption, like smoking, is a status offence in adolescence. The health risks may be objectively as real as those of smoking but have nothing like the same public salience. Nor does drinking attract the same social opprobrium as smoking; instead, it is still extensively promoted as a sociable, desirable and even glamorous activity. Moreover, it is regulated in quite different ways. And the dividing line between alcohol *use* and alcohol *abuse* is highly ambiguous.

Whatever the psychological mechanisms underlying alcohol abuse, therefore, there is no reason to expect that they will be the same as those for illegal drug use or for smoking. That said, the reasons that have been invoked for expecting low self-esteem to lead to alcohol abuse will now be familiar. These include the esteem enhancement argument – alcohol can, if temporarily, induce a more euphoric state and this will be especially attractive to people whose feelings of self-worth are

low. They also include the self-abuse argument – people who despise themselves will treat themselves badly. The social standing argument also arises here – those with low self-esteem have nothing further to lose from the disapproval their behaviour may attract.

Researchers most convinced of the truth of a particular hypothesis are those likely to look most energetically for the evidence to support their convictions. It is therefore instructive that R.A. Steffenhagen who has been one of the most consistent and vociferous advocates of the view that alcoholism results from low self-esteem has failed to find evidence to convince himself. Instead, he reports that depression is the most powerful predictor of alcoholism (e.g. Steffenhagen and Steffenhagen, 1985).

There is unfortunately a concealed problem in this apparently clear conclusion. Depression and low self-esteem are strongly related. Indeed, it is possible that measures of these two states are in reality measuring the same underlying quality. If so, then the statistical procedures for distinguishing the relative importance of depression and self-esteem will simply select the measure that does the better job of assessing this single underlying quality. The danger lies in assuming that one has measured two quite separate things when in reality only one thing has been measured, albeit in two different ways.

Whether or not Steffenhagen was misled in this way, however, the evidence that low self-esteem *leads to* alcohol abuse is not there (see Appendix, section on 'Alcohol abuse').

Risky sexual behaviour (including practices carrying risk of sexually transmitted diseases and of teenage pregnancy)

Young people who are self-esteeming are less likely to become pregnant as teenagers.
(California Task Force to Promote Self-esteem and Personal and Social Responsibility, 1990, p. 5)

23

Teenage pregnancy is different from the social problems so far considered in one significant respect. There is an event, pregnancy, which can be pinpointed in time. Consequently, it should in principle be possible to reach a clear conclusion here. Either prior low self-esteem predicts this event or it does not. Good longitudinal evidence – prospective studies – should on the face of it give us an unequivocal answer: the Task Force conclusion is either right or wrong.

In reality, of course, matters are not quite so simple. This is not just because 'less likely' could mean a whole lot less likely or a reduced probability of teenage pregnancy so small as to be devoid of practical significance. The lack of simplicity stems from the fact that the activity which brings pregnancy about is not effectively a single event. Rather, the probability that sexual intercourse leads to pregnancy increases among teenagers with age, with frequency of intercourse and as an inverse function of the efficacy of contraceptive measures. The probability may also increase with the number of sexual partners, over and above the effects of frequency of intercourse.

What need to be explained therefore are patterns of habitual behaviour, particularly frequency of intercourse, and adequacy of contraceptive behaviours. Given that these occupy spans of time and that their onset can be difficult to determine accurately, deciding which might come first, low self-esteem or the risky behaviours, becomes quite difficult. Nonetheless, untangling the sequence assumes even greater importance given the range of health risks that attend early, frequent, multi-partner and unprotected intercourse.

The theoretical arguments for expecting low self-esteem to increase the risk of teenage pregnancy and high self-esteem to decrease it are the familiar ones. But they also include embellishments specific to this case. One such is Luker's (1975) cost–benefit argument. It takes the notion that adolescents differ in their experiences and expectations of success. Low self-esteem is supposedly an expression of poor experiences and low expectations. Adolescents in this position will feel they have nothing to lose from becoming pregnant, that is, fewer costs. For example, there may be no expectation of academic success or rewarding employment which would otherwise be compromised by a pregnancy.

To this, Luker adds that there can be perceived costs to prevention. These could include but are not limited to the monetary cost of contraceptives themselves. Depending on the cultural climate there may be personal costs to the acquisition of contraceptives. Fortunately, in more enlightened times, the vital need to remove this particular barrier is increasingly recognised. But costs of rejection, of affection foregone, remain. Luker's analysis has several merits. But much of it could still hold even without a causal role for self-esteem.

Kaplan's esteem enhancement argument has also been invoked in various forms to explain teenage pregnancy. One view has it that adolescent girls can see motherhood as a more prestigious status than the one they currently occupy. Another is that pregnancy signals a move to the status of adult and an escape from a childhood status that has failed to provide feelings of self-worth. A third is that the sexual contact involved is associated with being loved and valued. As Crockenberg and Soby (1989) put it, sexual intercourse may 'validate the adolescent as an attractive person' (p. 131). And pregnancy would also validate capacity in a central biological role.

If any of these views has any virtue, then, there should be a gain in self-esteem from a sexual relationship or from pregnancy. Taking teenage pregnancy first, the lessons to be learned from comparisons of pregnant teenagers, teenagers who have become parents and teenagers who have experienced neither state are limited. One reason is that both teenage pregnancy and parenthood tend to attract strong social disapproval. To the extent that this is so, then diminished self-esteem could result from these conditions. Unpleasant physical symptoms associated with pregnancy could influence self-esteem scores. Additionally, the well-established phenomenon of post-natal depression complicates interpretations of evidence gathered from teenage mothers shortly after they have experienced childbirth.

Given these qualifications, what does research show? First, there does seem to be an association between low self-esteem and increased subsequent risk of pregnancy in adolescence (see Appendix, section on 'Sexual behaviour and teenage pregnancy'). However, just how this increased risk arises remains for the present unclear. With respect to contraception, we still await clear and persuasive evidence of the strength of any association between contraceptive use and self-esteem or decisive evidence that self-esteem is the causal factor in any such association. Moreover, the question begged should a causal influence be confirmed is the following: why would low self-esteem result in less effective contraception?

Several possibilities suggest themselves. Acquiring contraceptives requires self-esteem. One is more likely to use them consistently if one's sense of self-worth is high. One will be more successful in persuading sexual partners to take precautions. One will be less vulnerable to pressure from a partner to have unprotected sex. And so on. All these possibilities also remain to be verified, or ruled out.

To conclude, there is evidence for an increased risk – perhaps a 50 per cent increase – among teenage girls with lower self-esteem than their peers. The risk must arise because the former have more unprotected intercourse than the latter. Precisely why low self-esteem produces this effect remains, for the present, unclear. And, until we know this, we cannot know whether the risk can be reduced more effectively by raising self-esteem (the recommendation of the California Task Force) or through some other intervention such as targeted contraceptive advice and support.

Health risks and susceptibility to influence

As we have seen, a common theme in discussions of adolescent activities carrying a health risk is that young people are pressured into these activities by their peers. The recommended solution is to help youngsters develop the capacity to resist this kind of pressure. Health education campaigners and those who sponsor their campaigns have apparently long been convinced of the efficacy of this solution. So, young people are exhorted to 'say no' to drugs, cigarettes, alcohol, sexual advances, or any other proposition likely to endanger their health. And interventions intended to raise young people's self-esteem are often justified on the grounds that they will develop this kind of autonomy and immunity to peer pressure.

These ideas can claim some scientific authority. One quite widely used measure of self-esteem was developed to test the notion that persuasibility is a character trait, and that the essence of the trait is self-esteem. Irving Janis constructed this measure to test his prediction that people with low self-esteem would be more easily influenced than those with high self-esteem. And this is what he found (Janis and Field, 1959).

Given the conviction is so widespread that low self-esteem creates susceptibility to influence and to conformity pressures, it is worth taking a moment to examine the grounds for this conviction. It is worth doing because a great deal more evidence now exists about the connection between self-esteem and persuasibility. Moreover, a good meta-analysis of this evidence is available (Rhodes and Wood, 1992). Consequently, we are able to see not only whether there is a causal connection but also just how strong it is.

Rhodes and Wood (1992) found adequate tests of the connection in 57 separate pieces of research. They were also able to look at two kinds of potential effect, on the tendency to conform and on the tendency to be influenced. The latter was distinguished from the former by the presence of arguments supporting whatever was being advocated. Rhodes and Wood did find that there is a clear association between self-esteem and both conformity and influence. But it is not the association that might have been expected.

People with moderate, rather than either high or low, self-esteem show the greatest inclination to conform or to be influenced. The effect sizes were small to moderate. However, Rhodes and Wood also found indications that lows and highs show greater resistance to conformity and persuasion for different reasons. Lows, they suggest, have difficulty receiving the message. In other terms, they are less likely to notice what others are doing or that an attempt is being made to influence them. Highs, in contrast, do notice but reject the influence.

Two qualifications must be registered here. First, no effect of self-esteem was found for children (the authors of the analysis do not say precisely how they defined 'children' but it is possible this included all those below 18). Generally, there is much less evidence available on the self-esteem–influence link in adolescence. Second, virtually all of the available research is about conformity to or influence by strangers. In reality, most influence is likely to be exercised by acquaintances, and by family and friends in particular.

We may therefore still not have a clear answer to the question about social influence and its relation to self-esteem in adolescence. But the results of this analysis should cause us to re-examine two pervasive assumptions. One is that susceptibility to influence by others is necessarily a bad thing. The other is that it is sensible to explore only the possible consequences of high versus low self-esteem.

The idea that it is bad to conform and good to be independent is almost as old as the social sciences. Ever since Gustav Le Bon wrote his immensely popular book on the psychology of the crowd towards the end of the nineteenth century (Le Bon, 1896), the idea that going along with the crowd is a kind of weakness has suffused both the popular imagination and academic writings. Arguably, this can lead to the ridiculous and untenable position that every individual should make up his or her own mind about everything, should act independently in every way and should never concur with the opinions of others.

A more reasonable position, I believe, is that it is healthy and adaptive to take into account the opinions of others when deciding one's own opinion (cf. Emler and Reicher, 1995). Moreover, the influence of others is more likely to be benign and constructive than negative, and sensitivity to this influence is more likely to result in responsible behaviour and sensible choices than publicly costly or personally damaging actions. If young people do show an inclination to go along with their peers in many things, this is more often than not a force for the good.

If this position is reasonable, then it may also be the case that the optimal level of self-esteem is not high. If self-esteem is a favourable opinion of oneself, then people with very high self-esteem will also sometimes be described in less positive terms – overbearing, arrogant, self-centred, narcissistic, egotistic, smug, vain. The results of the Rhodes and Wood analysis should set alarm bells ringing. If self-esteem has benefits, researchers may have been looking in the wrong places for them. Those benefits may lie in moderation and not at either extreme.

Child maltreatment

… child battering mothers [are] usually young, have immature dependent personalities, lack self-esteem. (Mitchell, 1975, p. 641)

The view that parents with low self-esteem are more likely to abuse their children is commonplace in the medical profession. And, if true, it would indicate a worryingly toxic process in which the damaged self-esteem of one generation transmits similar damage to the next. For there are strong indications, as we shall see later, that victims of child abuse have diminished self-esteem as adolescents and adults.

There are two limitations in particular to the available research (see Appendix, section on 'Child abuse'). First, there is very little of it and the samples have been small. Second, almost all the research so far published compares parents already identified as abusers with others considered to be non-abusing parents. The latter category is likely to include some – indeed an unknown number – of unidentified abusers. This approach inevitably raises a question about any observed association between abusive parenting and low self-esteem.

This is clearly one social problem that would benefit from more research to discover its roots. Genuinely informative research will not be easy, for the reasons outlined above. But, if it is to be undertaken, there is also a case for considering possibilities beyond the damaging effects of low self-esteem. Baumeister and his colleagues (Baumeister *et al.*, 1996) provide a strong argument that violence of all kinds, including violent abuse of one's own children, is more likely to be done by people whose self-esteem is very high than by those whose self-esteem is rather low. They point out that the former category will include people whose high opinion of themselves will be more often challenged. This will be especially true when that high opinion has little basis in reality.

Educational underachievement

No single aspect of self-esteem has attracted quite so much research attention as its relation to education. One source of interest reflects the suspicion that educational failure damages young people's self-esteem. The other principal possibility to have aroused this attention is that self-esteem itself plays some role in educational attainment. Specifically do children fail in part because their self-esteem is low?

The most important direct determinant of educational attainment is ability. But equally clearly it is not the whole story. Measured ability on entry to formal education does not explain all of the variance in eventual achievements. Given that the association between initial ability and achievement is imperfect, therefore, what causes some children to 'overachieve' – to do better than their intellectual ability would suggest they should – and others to underachieve relative to their intellectual potential?

There have been many candidates for the role of extra ingredient here and self-esteem is just one. But it has also been viewed as a potential mediator of other factors such as social background – in effect as the proximal cause through which more remote influences work. And it has been seen as a moderator, amplifying or dampening the impact of such variables as degree of parental support.

Over many years of research, a consistent pattern is apparent. Self-esteem and educational attainment are related. But they are not strongly related. The strength of the association varies with age; with the educational outcome considered; with the sex, ethnic origin and socio-economic background of the individuals concerned; and with the measures of self-esteem used. The correlations in individual studies have occasionally been as high as 0.5 (West *et al.*, 1980). But on average they are lower, much lower. A review by Hansford and Hattie (1982) estimated the strength of the correlation at 0.16. West *et al.* (1980), examining findings from around 300 studies, put the estimate at 0.18.

A number of longitudinal studies in this area have provided the opportunity to see whether this association actually reflects the influence of self-esteem on subsequent educational attainments. It does not (e.g. Hoge *et al.*, 1995). The weak relationship that was consistently found reflects a small effect of attainment on self-esteem and not the reverse.

Recent analysis of data from a major longitudinal study in Britain confirms the weak effects of earlier self-esteem on later educational attainment. Feinstein (2000) analysed data from the 1970 British Cohort Study, which included a measure of self-esteem taken at age ten. With respect to subsequent educational qualifications, he was able to consider information from just under 8,500 members of the cohort. Self-esteem was only trivially related to later educational attainments in this sample.

The considerable volume of research devoted to this single question has revealed much about both the nature of self-esteem and the non-intellectual influences on educational attainment. But it has not substantially altered this conclusion. One consequence has been to focus attention on the role of education-specific self-esteem. Numerous measures of this are now in use. Furthermore, they do relate more strongly to attainment than global measures. But to argue that explanation lies in domain-specific forms of self-esteem is something very different.

One interesting discovery is that level of global self-esteem does not have much impact on what young people want or try to achieve in this domain. It does, however, influence what they expect to achieve. McFarlin and Blaskovich (1981) demonstrated that people with low self-esteem wanted to succeed as much as anyone else. They also tried just as hard. But unlike people with high self-esteem they expected to fail. However, because performance is influenced by effort rather than by expectations of success or failure, there are few differences in the achievements of low- and high-esteem individuals.

One other curious difference is that people with high self-esteem can show greater persistence at a task but in such a way that results in no consistent advantage. This is because the persistence is often counterproductive; it can be wasted effort on lost causes (McFarlin *et al.*, 1984).

Chronic dependency on state support (including poverty, low earnings and long-term unemployment)

Americans seem politically especially sensitised to the evils of what they call chronic welfare dependency. In other countries, the condition at issue might more simply be labelled 'poverty'. But describing the condition as welfare dependency – or dependency on state support – puts the spotlight on the individual who occupies this condition and not, for example, on the circumstances of the labour market or structural features intrinsic to a free-market, capital and labour economy. It invites us to look at the character of this individual to understand the condition.

It does not mandate any particular answer. Nevertheless, among the options are explanations which hold the individual culpable, guilty of laziness, limited imagination or cynical exploitation of the system. In this context, low self-esteem is one of the more sympathetic options. It also suggests its own solution: nobody wants to be dependent on state handouts and those who are can be helped to escape by first raising their self-esteem.

We do not have to accept the question as posed here. It was on the California Task Force list of social problems and owes its presence to the political requirements of selling the rest of the Task Force agenda to the state government. Ironically, also, the scale of this particular 'social problem' is much smaller in the United States than it is in Britain and other west European countries. In 1984, just prior to the creation of the Task Force, the United States was spending under 0.4 per cent of its gross national product on what could be called welfare handouts – in California itself, the percentage was much lower still (Schneiderman *et al.*, 1989). And it was already on a downward trend.

None of this reduces the capacity for newspapers to sell copy that pillories 'welfare scroungers' or for politicians to find a sympathetic audience for their concerns about the burden of welfare borne by hard-working taxpayers. Refugees labelled as economic migrants currently arouse the same fears and grievances as unmarried mothers did before these new suspects appeared on the scene. So, is there any solid scientific evidence that poverty or its consequences for dependency on state financial support have their roots, even if only in part, in low self-esteem?

The grounds for this explanation are similar to those for the role of low self-esteem in educational failure. People with low self-esteem have low expectations for success and consequently fail to make the best use of the talents they have. They feel more helpless than they should in the face of their circumstances and so do not make appropriate efforts to change them.

However persuasive any of this sounds in theory, there is as yet very little evidence to substantiate it. Schneiderman and his co-authors, charged with writing the review for this item on the Task Force agenda, instead offered a lesson in the real causes of poverty and the real costs of welfare dependency. As for self-esteem, they conclude thus:

The widely held assumption that low self-esteem has predictable behavioral consequences that are necessarily associated with low motivation or lack of initiative or social responsibility is not supported by the empirical literature.
(Schneiderman et al., 1989, p. 223)

They go on to note that the relevant evidence if anything supports completely the opposite conclusion.

Their scepticism about any negative consequences of low self-esteem may have been premature. Most of the research capable of illuminating the question does indeed support their view (see Appendix, section on 'Economic consequences'). However, one very recent analysis

of data from a British sample (Feinstein, 2000) clearly indicates strong influences of childhood self-esteem on outcomes in adulthood, specifically whether or not young men experienced extended periods of unemployment and how much they were earning by their mid-twenties (interestingly, there were quite different long-term consequences of childhood self-esteem for females). This may be only one study but it is based on a very substantial sample and it cannot easily be dismissed. The challenge now must be to explain how and why childhood self-esteem has these economic consequences.

Eating disorders

In the light of the publicity surrounding eating disorders, it might come as a surprise that the prevalence rates for these disorders is actually very low. For anorexia, it has been estimated at between one and two in 1,000 for females and about ten times less for males (Fombonne, 1995). Bulimia, which has only more recently been recognised as a distinct disorder, has according to Fombonne a higher rate at around 2 per cent for women. Again, the incidence for males is about one-tenth of that for females.

Given these rates, it is tempting to conclude that although eating disorders represent personal troubles they do not qualify as social problems. However, less stringent criteria than those applied for clinical diagnosis of a disorder indicate substantially higher rates for various symptoms of eating pathology, such as binge eating, self-induced vomiting, laxative misuse, inappropriate dieting, unhealthy weight loss and excessive, food-related exercise. At the same time, on any measure of eating dysfunction, females are more often the sufferers than males.

In Fombonne's (1995) review of possible causal mechanisms underlying eating disturbances, covering the literature up to around 1992, no mention is made of self-esteem as a possible factor. But, prior to that date, hardly anyone seems to have considered the possibility. Since then, there has been a veritable explosion of studies examining this particular risk factor. And, in virtually every case, a connection has been found. It does not follow, however, that low self-esteem is a risk factor for the development of eating disorders.

Various reasons have been advanced for an association between low self-esteem and eating disorders. The most popular is that eating is disordered in individuals who are unhappy with something about themselves, in this case their body shape or weight or appearance. Because low self-esteem entails dissatisfaction with the self, it may therefore extend to anything seen to be associated with all or part of the self, including the body. This could be taken to imply that dissatisfaction with one's body is one consequence of a more generalised dissatisfaction with oneself. Alternatively, it could mean that people's general sense of their own worth is the sum of their views about a number of distinguishable aspects of themselves and their bodies are among these aspects.

If this latter is the case, then what needs to be explained is why some people are so dissatisfied with their bodies that they are constantly trying to change them. Knowing about their self-esteem would make no contribution to such an explanation because it is a consequence – or part expression – of this dissatisfaction, not a cause. If the former interpretation is the more appropriate, then we need also to pay careful attention to the way in which self-esteem is measured. Some aggregate measures of self-esteem include as one of the aggregated components evaluations of the body. Finding that people who evaluate their bodies negatively also, for example, diet to excess is not telling us very much.

A different kind of interpretation treats eating disorders as forms of self-abuse. One consequence of a negative attitude is that the object of this attitude is treated badly. Yet another is that low self-esteem increases the likelihood of actions which are essentially consolations, temporary escapes from an unhappy condition. But if, for example, binge eating is a consoling pleasure of this kind, the consolations of severe dieting are less obvious. If either of these interpretations are appropriate, then self-esteem should be associated with some eating disorders but not others – in the first case those that are self-destructive, in the second those that are self-indulgent. What does the evidence show?

In this case, there does appear to be a link between low self-esteem and the subsequent appearance or development of problem behaviours (see Appendix, section on 'Eating disorders'). Indeed, research has now moved on to inquiries into the mechanisms underlying this link. However, a perhaps realistic conclusion for the present is that self-esteem has *an* influence on eating disorders, but that it is just one among several factors affecting the occurrence and course of these disorders. This conclusion also seems appropriate in the light of Veron-Guidry *et al.*'s (1997) study of eight to 13 year olds in which low self-esteem emerged as just one among a number of risk factors here.

Suicide, parasuicide and suicidal thoughts

According to Rittner and Smyth (1999), suicide is the third leading cause of death among US adolescents, after accidents and homicides. In many other countries, it is the second most frequent cause of death in this age group. It is certainly a sufficiently serious matter to have attracted extensive attention from the World Health Organization. But it is also a relatively uncommon occurrence. One of the highest national rates recorded is for Hungary with an annual rate of 600 per million males or 0.06 per cent. For Britain, the overall rate is around 0.015 per cent. It is also an event related to age; it is least common among children and most common among adults. It is therefore not conspicuously a problem of youth (though in the UK the rate for males aged 25 to 44 has recently overtaken that for older men). Finally, rates everywhere seem to be lower among females, partly because males tend to use more lethal methods.

The low incidence of suicide makes it particularly difficult to study, and perhaps by virtue of its rarity there are hardly any prospective studies. A sample of 10,000 young people might contain one individual who will complete a suicide attempt in any one year. This rarity has also favoured attention to phenomena thought to be related, such as suicide attempts and thoughts about suicide.

As regards attempts, some researchers prefer the term 'parasuicide' (cf. Kreitman, 1977) for deliberate acts that could have resulted in the death of the individual concerned. This term is preferred to 'suicide attempt' on the grounds that the intentions surrounding the action will often be difficult to determine and may not even be apparent to the person who makes the attempt. Suicidal thoughts, or 'suicidal ideation', refers to 'thoughts implying a desire, intention, to end life by one's own hand' (Diekstra *et al.*, 1995, p. 688), though many studies assessing such thoughts have used looser definitions.

A further advantage of studying parasuicide and suicidal ideation is that those concerned are still alive to be studied. The disadvantage is that observations of people who have been identified as making suicide attempts or thinking regularly about suicide are potentially observations about the consequences of such identification and not the causes of these thoughts or actions. A further problem is the validity of the assumption that parasuicides or people with suicidal thoughts are similar to successful suicides – their thoughts and behaviour will be driven by the same factors – and differ only in that they have not yet succeeded or

reached the extremes that will produce more lethal consequences. Are the differences therefore really just a matter of degree?

Many investigations, whether of suicides, parasuicides, or suicidal ideation, have considered low self-esteem as a risk factor, perhaps for reasons too obvious to state. The only surprise might be in finding that low self-esteem was quite unrelated to any of these phenomena. Research has yet to provide such a surprise. On the other hand, simply demonstrating that one variable quality – self-esteem – is correlated with occurrence of any of the outcomes is virtually useless.

The reason why discovery of a simple association between self-esteem and any suicide-related outcome will be, in the absence of any other information, uninformative is that these outcomes are associated with a wide range of factors. Moreover, at least some of these factors, most obviously depression, are themselves related to self-esteem. Thus, minimally, one wants to know not just whether self-esteem is associated with the outcomes, and beyond that whether such an association reflects a causal influence of self-esteem, but also how important this causal influence is compared to the many other potential causal influences.

This being so, informative research will assess several potential risk factors at the same time and will employ statistical procedures with the capacity to separate out their respective independent effects if any.

The conclusions with respect to suicide, and thoughts and actions related to suicide must be as tentative as those for eating disorders (see Appendix, section on 'Suicide, suicide attempts and suicidal thoughts'). On the one hand, there is a strong case for concluding that negative feelings about the self increase the risk of these outcomes and these negative feelings are part of what is captured by some measures of self-esteem. On the other hand, there are many other quite independent risk factors. What we do not yet know, and will not know until more evidence from sufficiently well-designed studies is available, is the relative importance of these feelings as risk factors. Nor do we yet know whether they mediate the impact of some other factors, or whether they amplify the risk in combination with particular other factors.

Outcomes: overview

The available research supports the following conclusions about the role of low self-esteem in the social problems listed earlier.

With respect to a range of problems, no impact of low self-esteem is apparent. That is to say, the patterns of behaviour constituting or contributing to the problem cannot be attributed to lack of self-esteem. These problems include:

- crime, including violent crime

- racial prejudice

- teenage smoking

- child maltreatment.

In the case of racial prejudice, high self-esteem rather than low appears to be related to the outcome. In the case of violence, there are some indications that *high* self-esteem in combination with other factors carries a risk.

There is a second category of problems for which the influence of low self-esteem is not proven or its influence is very slight (the 'not proven' cases may merit further attention):

- educational underachievement

- alcohol abuse

- drug abuse.

With respect to four problems, low self-esteem does appear to be a risk factor. These are:

- teenage pregnancy and possibly unprotected sexual contact carrying a risk of sexually transmitted infection

- eating disorders

- suicide attempts, whether or not successful, and suicidal thoughts

- low earnings and extended unemployment (males).

In each of these cases, it is also evident, however, that low self-esteem is one among a number of risk factors and the indications are that, apart from the risk for females of teenage pregnancy and for males of extended unemployment and lower earnings in their twenties, its impact is relatively minor. It would be productive to focus further research in each case upon the ways in which self-esteem interacts with other risk factors. The following questions in particular remain to be resolved:

1 Does self-esteem mediate the impact of certain of the other risk factors? If it can be shown to do so, then we would be in a better position to decide whether interventions should be directed at these more remote causes or at breaking the impact they have on low self-esteem

2 Does self-esteem operate as a risk factor quite independently of any others and, if so, to what extent does it affect risk compared to the other factors? If we can determine this more precisely, we are in a better position to decide whether resources should be focused upon this risk factor rather than others. Such a decision, however, should also consider the relative costs of alternative interventions.

3 Does self-esteem amplify or moderate the impact of other risk factors? If this can be determined, we will be in a better position to decide which of the factors, self-esteem or those others with which it interacts, is the more appropriate focus for intervention.

At this point, one might ask why low self-esteem does not have a wider range of negative effects. Or, rather, why has it not been possible to identify negative effects in so many of the areas considered? Has the science for some reason failed us because it does not confirm what intuition and common experience tell us is true?

The most obvious way in which it might have failed is in its detection of the presence of low self-esteem. In other words, the methods of measurement have been inappropriate or insufficiently sensitive. It is true that some researchers, notably Greenwald and Banaji (1995), have strongly criticised the methods most widely used to assess self-esteem. The substance of their criticism is that methods in which people answer direct questions about their feelings towards themselves are more likely to detect what people are prepared to claim about their feelings than about the true character of these feelings. Answers will reflect either beliefs about what is the socially desirable thing to say, or the degree to which a person is prepared to be modest or boastful about themselves.

It has yet to be shown that the alternative method of measurement advocated by Greenwald and Banaji can satisfy the basic requirements of precision and validity, or that any of the other alternatives – such as observers' ratings – can do so. There is also a question about the practicality of these alternatives, particularly in large-scale research with young people. But these problems are beside the point. If Greenwald and Banaji are right, then the facts that a widely employed measure such as Rosenberg's scale is practical to use and that it achieves a high level of precision are not adequate justifications for its use.

On the other side of the argument, one can ask: does the pattern of findings make sense? I think that, very largely, they do make sense and in the next chapter, where I look at the determinants of self-esteem, the justification for this confidence will, I hope, become clearer. But, to anticipate, the pattern indicates the following: *people who have, or admit to, negative feelings about themselves also treat themselves badly (and may be badly treated by others). They do not tend to treat others badly.*

The apparent anomalies of drug abuse, alcohol abuse and cigarette smoking are less anomalous if one considers that (a) the 'abusers' are not primarily intent on self-harm and (b) they may be aware of health risks in their habits but their risk taking stems from confidence, however unrealistic, that they can beat the odds; these activities do not stem from lack of confidence. Pelham (1993), for example, reports that young adults with high self-esteem are the ones more likely to take up risky pursuits, such as riding motorcycles, and to take greater risks in these, such as driving too fast and driving while under the influence of alcohol.

The pattern also makes sense once one recognises (anticipating evidence reviewed in Chapter 3) that there is little connection between having positive or negative feelings about oneself on the one hand and one's objective accomplishments or failures on the other.

Greenwald is undoubtedly right that the commonly used measures of self-esteem detect differences in what people are prepared publicly to admit or claim about themselves. But it does not follow that these admissions or claims bear no relation to what they privately feel. What we can learn from this observation, however, is something quite informative about self-esteem. It partly describes how people behave publicly; it describes what they are and are not willing to say about themselves to others. Consequently, we should ask:

1   Why are some people willing to admit that they think themselves worthless?

2   What are the consequences of this kind of public admission?

Answers to both will be considered in the next chapter. But, to anticipate those to the second question, if you tell others you have no value, you are inviting them to treat you as if this were true.

This admission therefore carries a risk of victimisation.

One other way in which the science may have failed is in the detection of relatively hidden influences of low self-esteem. These influences could be hidden if self-esteem primarily operated as a moderator of the impact of other factors. This would be the case, for example, if low self-esteem, compared to high, increased levels of alcohol abuse among young people also exposed to high levels of stress, but decreased these levels among those not exposed to stresses. The influence could also be hidden if, for example, low self-esteem in combination with a deferential attitude to authority produced educational underachievement and if this effect also resulted from *high* self-esteem combined with a *hostile* attitude to authority.

I have already noted that moderator effects can be harder to spot. Moreover, despite their potential importance, in few studies have they been systematically investigated or ruled out. There may therefore be a case for considering such effects in future research. But, if the necessary effort is to be expended, there should be a reasonable and reasoned presumption as to where these effects will be found. This requires an informed understanding of what differences in self-esteem are and how they arise. I turn next, therefore, to these questions.

3 The sources of differences in self-esteem

The scientific search for the determinants of self-esteem has been guided by the various theories as to its nature. The view of William James (1890) that self-esteem is success divided by pretensions potentially directs the search to two places. Does self-esteem result primarily from the degree to which a person succeeds in their aspirations? Alternatively, does it depend primarily upon the nature of those aspirations? Both possibilities have been explored. Cooley's (1902) emphasis on the perceived or anticipated reactions of others might seem to suggest that experience of others' disapproval, or experience of hostility, rejection or stigmatisation by others will lead those who experience these reactions to devalue themselves. In fact, much attention has been given to the consequences of belonging to low status categories.

What has emerged about the roots of self-esteem is not entirely what was anticipated. And this is leading to a reappraisal of the nature of self-esteem. Many of the factors which might be expected to result in low self-esteem do not do so. I will consider in turn: factors that have weak effects or none; factors that have modest effects; factors that have a more significant impact.

Factors that have weak effects or none

Ethnicity or race

Given that membership of a racial or ethnic minority so frequently results in exposure to rejection, abuse, discrimination and persecution, such membership carries with it a clear message that one is not valued by the majority culture. The impact of this kind of experience on self-esteem is very clear. It has none.

The relation between ethnic identity and self-esteem has been studied extensively. A recent review of the research literature identified 261 studies comparing the self-esteem of black and white Americans (Gray-Little and Hafdahl, 2000). The authors of the review were able to determine not only whether this research indicated any difference between the two groups but, using the techniques of meta-analysis, the precise size of the difference. The research reviewed covered children, adolescents and adults.

In every age group except the youngest, the average self-esteem of black Americans was not lower than that of whites; it was higher. The difference is not large but it is highly consistent. It is present among both males and females and it increases with age.

It is possible that black Americans are a special group and that their self-esteem owes something to a shared culture, which has vigorously and successfully promoted the status of black identity. The authors of the review suggest that other ethnic groups in America, such as Hispanics, may not show this advantage. The implication is that they belong to a less cohesive culture, which has collectively done less to promote its distinctive virtues.

It is also possible that the meaning of responses to self-esteem measures varies across cultures. If the cultural norms prescibe modesty then the members of that culture may be less inclined to claim that they are highly worthy people. If a degree of boasting or aggressive self-promotion is culturally approved, self-esteem scores could be higher. Is this, for example, why the self-esteem scores of Caribbean adolescents are higher than those of Indian adolescents (Richardson, 1987)?

These possibilities should be taken seriously, but there are also good theoretical grounds for concluding that membership of an ethnic minority will in itself have no adverse effect on self-esteem. Crocker and Major (1989) spell out three reasons why self-esteem is not damaged by membership of a stigmatised group:

- The negative reactions to which they are exposed are attributed to prejudice. The fault is located in the person who reacts and not in the target of their negative reaction.

- Minority group members do not directly compare their circumstances with those of higher status groups. Their social comparisons are made with other members of their own group.

- Minority groups reject the value of the qualities they supposedly lack. So, for example, if their persecutors allege lack of academic competence, the relevance of this particular quality will be discounted and other qualities will be emphasised, for example athletic talent.

Gray-Little and Hafdahl (2000) suggest a fourth reason:

- The approval that matters most to people and that has the greatest impact on their self-esteem is the approval of those close to them, their family and friends, and not the approval of strangers or of a wider society.

Each of these reasons has a sound basis in research (extensively reviewed by the authors cited above). But their relevance is not restricted to the consequences of ethnic identity.

Social class

Social class membership carries some of the same implications for personal identity as ethnic group identity. Because social classes correspond to an order of status and prestige, and because they carry implications of relative social value, a person's position in the class structure might be expected to have consequences for their view of their own personal worth. However, position in the class structure differs from ethnic identity in at least one important respect. Whereas people cannot change their race or skin colour, it is implied that they can alter their own social class position. Aspirations to upward mobility are regarded as both appropriate and realistic. Correspondingly, if one occupies a

lowly position, the implication is that one lacks the wit or talent or application necessary to have escaped it. Class position therefore seems to carry a different and perhaps clearer message about one's relative worth as a person.

Social class position is linked to adult self-esteem (e.g. Rosenberg and Pearlin, 1978) but only modestly. One reason for this is that level of self-esteem in adulthood is already substantially determined in adolescence. The same study shows that adolescent and childhood levels of self-esteem are not related to social class position. Rosenberg and Pearlin argue this is because class position is an acquired or inherited status for children and adolescents, one derived from their parents' position. It therefore carries no direct implications for their own worth or lack of it. Later, I will consider why adults are not more affected by a status that is for them apparently an achieved position.

Wiltfang and Scarbecz (1990) used data from a large-scale study of American adolescents, the Richmond Youth Project, to check on Rosenberg and Pearlin's conclusions about this age group. This project is based on a sample of some 4,000 young people aged 12 to 19. Wiltfang and Scarbecz found that the self-esteem of the teenagers in this study was quite unrelated to father's occupation, the traditional indicator of social class position.

They also, however, explored the possibility of other 'hidden injuries' of social class. Their analysis revealed three such injuries to self-esteem: father's education; whether or not the father was unemployed; and perceived levels of unemployment in the neighbourhood. It should be added that, although each of these effects was statistically significant, in such a large sample this will be true even of very small effects. These were small effects which together accounted for little more than 5 per cent of the overall differences in self-esteem within the sample.

Gender

Entering adolescence as spirited and self confident girls, the subjects of the study often emerged as defeated young women lacking a belief in themselves and their abilities.
(John Hewitt, 1998, p. 6, summarising the conclusions to emerge from the study 'Shortchanging girls, shortchanging America')

In 1991, the American Association of University Women (AAUW) launched a campaign to promote the view that the system was severely damaging the self-esteem of adolescent girls. In the view of the campaigners, the damage was not a product of any general stigmatisation of females in society. It did not result from cultural attitudes that women as a category have lower status than men. Rather, it reflected the demoralising personal experiences of most girls as they moved through the education system.

The AAUW had a clear view that women do lack self-esteem compared to men and also a clear view as to how this comes about. Nonetheless, other arguments can be adduced for such a difference (cf. Kling *et al.*, 1999). One is that the gender roles for males and females prescribe different qualities. Boys are encouraged to be assertive and self-promoting, girls are not; in other words, girls, compared to boys, are not encouraged to make strong claims about their self-worth. Another is that boys and girls develop, within the single-sex peer groups that dominate childhood, different interpersonal strategies. When they do interact in mixed-sex groups, the strategies developed by boys tend to prevail, leaving girls feeling less competent, important or powerful. Differences in the size and body strength of males and females might lead one to the conclusion that females will more often be the victims of male physical violence than the reverse. This also could have damaging effects on their self-esteem.

There are, indeed, several arguments leading to the conclusion that the self-esteem of women will be lower than that of men. But, before considering the relative merits of these as explanations, we should ask whether there is a difference to explain. Fortunately, the question has been examined extensively and meta-analysis allows clear conclusions about the scale of the difference.

Kling and colleagues (1999) identified 216 studies of gender differences in self-esteem in which sufficient information was available to estimate the size of the difference. Males score higher on measures of global self-esteem. The difference is highly consistent, but it is also small. One factor influencing the size of the difference is age. The largest differences are apparent in late adolescence; they are smaller both before and after.

One problem this leaves for the explanations of gender differences considered above is that collectively they would appear to over-explain the difference. It is considerably less than one would anticipate if all these explanations were appropriate. The alternative is that only some of these explanations apply and/or that the consequences they anticipate are partly countered in other ways. Moreover, there may be circumstances specific to the experience of males that disproportionately damage their self-esteem. For example, if athletic prowess or muscularity are attributes more valued in males than in females, then boys but not girls who lack them might suffer loss of self-esteem. Later, I will consider factors influencing self-esteem that are likely to affect males and females differentially.

Finally, is a small difference necessarily also a *trivial* difference? The overall 'effect size' as estimated by Kling *et al.* was 0.21. One useful way of deciding what this means in practice is to consider its implications for selection. It means that if, for example, males and females were selected for jobs in a way that perfectly reflected their respective self-esteem scores (not in reality remotely the case), ten more males out of every 100 would be selected for the job than females. Clearly, this is not a trivial difference.

Kling and her colleagues also pose the question: what might the cumulative effects of such a difference be? Career success, for example, may be the cumulative consequence of a succession of decisions taken over many years from primary school onwards. If self-esteem influences each of those decisions, the ultimate effect of a 'small' gender difference in self-esteem could be a large difference in career outcome. On the other hand, the effects of self-esteem on each of these choices could be small. An effect size of 0.21 for self-esteem differences between males and females will almost certainly not translate into the same effect size for differences in the choices they make. And further caution is suggested by the narrowing differences in male versus female attainments, both educational and occupational.

Factors that have a modest effect

Successes and failures
Real successes should raise self-esteem. Real failures should lower self-esteem. A history of continual success should secure permanently high self-esteem. Experience of continual failure should result in chronic low self-esteem. These assumptions are embedded not just in popular suppositions about self-esteem but in much of the scientific thinking about the phenomenon. They also underlie several measures of self-esteem, which essentially assess people's beliefs about their successes and failures, their assets and liabilities. It is tempting to suppose that these perceptions and beliefs are shaped quite directly by realities. But are they?

Experimental research, in which the objective is to manipulate levels of self-esteem and observe the effects, commonly uses the ploy of giving participants false feedback on their performance. Typically, they will take a test or perform a task and then be told either that they have succeeded (or done very well compared to the average) or that they have failed (or done poorly compared to the

average). Self-esteem does appear temporarily to rise or fall depending on the feedback. However, the tasks used tend, whether explicitly or by implication, to require intellectual competence. The participants in these studies are almost invariably college students. And one might suppose that a sense of intellectual competence will be more than usually central to the self-worth of such people. The feedback threatens, or endorses, a belief that is particularly important to them. Would other kinds of people care equally about their performance of such tasks?

However, it is perhaps more pertinent to show that successes and failures have more than short-term effects. The assumption that this is the case is the logic for some measures of self-esteem. So-called aggregate measures presuppose that a person's self-esteem is based on a kind of audit of their successes and failures in various domains. The results of this audit are added together, either in the mind of the individual or through the scoring procedure for the measure, to produce an overall or summary self-esteem.

One really wants to know two things here. First, how objective or at least how unbiased are people's estimates of their own successes and failures? Second, is their overall sense of their own worth – their global self-esteem – really built up through mental aggregation of these estimates? Can we assume an inference is made from 'good at X' to 'good/worthy person'? In neither case does the answer turn out to be straightforward.

There is a general bias towards inflated estimates of one's own excellence in any area of human activity in which particular qualities of performance are culturally valued. So, for example, a majority of people are convinced that their sense of humour is superior to the average. Similarly, most people believe their own driving skills are better than those of the average driver. Judgements of such matters are fallible, therefore, but it does not follow that judgements are also invariably wrong on a *relative* scale. The worst driver may think he is just above the population average, the best may believe himself far superior to this average. Consequently, self-evaluations and self-esteem could still be sensibly related to objective differences in performance.

The relationship is, however, far less perfect than should be the case if people really do derive their self-evaluations from their performances. This is particularly true of valued qualities that lack clear and objective standards of evaluation, such as qualities of personality and character. People's own estimates of their relative standing with respect to a range of personal virtues agree only imperfectly with the estimates their acquaintances make of them (Kenny, 1994; Taylor and Brown, 1988).

There are, however, areas of activity in which performance standards are more explicit and relative performance levels are routinely published. It is not only professional tennis players who are exposed to public rankings. Every schoolchild is regularly measured against classmates; all know just how well they are doing relative to every other child in the class and, ultimately, where they stand in achievement relative to national averages. In such areas of performance, it is hard to see how self-evaluations could not reflect achievements.

But another step is required to link achievements to self-esteem. Moreover, this step is not necessarily present if aggregate measures are used to assess self-esteem. A person could honestly and accurately evaluate themselves as physically unco-ordinated, lacking in academic accomplishments and bereft of musical talent, and also remain convinced that they are of great worth. Furthermore, this does happen and to a considerable extent. People's feeling about themselves, their global sense of self-worth, is only modestly influenced by their actual accomplishments and imperfectly related to their own estimates of these.

The effects of academic achievement upon self-esteem have received particular attention and so there is no longer much room for doubt about

either the existence of these effects or their extent. Comprehensive reviews of the evidence have appeared regularly since the 1960s and all tell the same story. Research consistently finds an association between academic achievements, however measured, and self-esteem. We have already considered this evidence in looking at the possible effects of low self-esteem on educational underachievement. And we saw that there were no strong grounds for attributing this association to the effects of self-esteem on academic performance.

The research is also very consistent in its conclusion that the association is rather small. West *et al.* (1980) found, reviewing around 100 studies, an average correlation of 0.18. To take a single example, the Wiltfang and Scarbecz (1990) analysis of the Richmond Youth Project evidence produced an estimate for the correlation between school grades and self-esteem of around 0.17. So, taking more optimistic estimates, the implications are that if achievement in school were the same for everyone the amount by which self-esteem varied in the population would be reduced by about 4 per cent. What explains the remaining 96 per cent?

Actually, it is unlikely the figure to be explained is 96 per cent, or that this amount of variation ever could be explained. The figure assumes that self-esteem has been measured without any error at all. It is rather more likely that the degree of error in measurement is between 25 and 40 per cent. If this seems alarmingly high, it is not unusual for psychological measures of this kind. As noted earlier, measurement precision can be increased but at a cost. A more sensible option is to take the measurement error into account when deciding how much we have understood about the causes of variations in self-esteem.

Before turning to other possible causes, it is instructive to consider why achievement does not have more impact on self-esteem. Part of the reason seems to be that there are options for explaining performance that have few implications for one's worth as a person. A poor performance can be attributed to bad luck, lack of effort or a biased teacher unwilling to give good marks. In the longer run, additional tactics are available. Poor memory helps. Poor performances are forgotten and only good ones remembered. Even if the poorer performances are recalled, they can be remembered as rather better than they actually were. Optimism also helps. Unrealistic expectations are sustained about future performances even though past ones have been poor.

The greater puzzle perhaps is why some people will discount good performances to protect a view of themselves as worthless? Yet it does seem that the nature of these biases reflects self-esteem. Those blessed with high self-esteem ignore all evidence of inadequacies. Those who lack esteem equally consistently deny that there is any positive evidence, using many of the same tactics in reverse. Successes are attributed to luck or overly sympathetic examiners; only failures are remembered with any accuracy and the future is expected to be bleak.

Even so, Brown and McGill's (1989) finding that good outcomes can actually damage the health of those with low self-esteem is surprising. They found in two studies, respectively of high school and college students, that those who had low self-esteem and experienced high levels of positive life events – a number of good things happened to them (such as addition of a new family member or the start of a new relationship)[1] – subsequently displayed more symptoms of illness. It is as if, having concluded that you are worthless, strong evidence to the contrary is distressing and difficult to manage.

At least one authority on the development of self-esteem, Susan Harter (1998), has argued that we need to take William James more seriously here, in the following respect. What matters is not just how successful you are, but what kinds of success you want – James's 'pretensions'. Harter reports

that the relation between self-esteem and competence in areas that a person regards as important is far stronger than the relation in areas judged unimportant. This only helps, however, if it can be shown that these judgements of what matters precede evidence of performance. Otherwise, it is entirely possible, as others have proposed, that this is just another tactic to preserve an already adopted view of the self.

To decide between these possibilities, Harter does a strange thing. Whether self-esteem determines what you value or whether it works the other way around is a key issue. Research evidence that could settle it would be extremely valuable. Instead, Harter asks adolescents which alternative they think is more likely. It turns out that a moderate majority believe their self-esteem is shaped by qualities they see as particularly important (the quality actually considered here was appearance – young people, and particularly girls, claim their own physical appearance is highly important to them).

There is now sufficient evidence of people's willingness and ability to deceive themselves to suggest that beliefs in this case are not a sound guide to what is really going on. On the other side, there is good evidence that people perceive the things they are not good at as less important and do so precisely because they are not good at these things. Even so, Harter still may be partly right but it would help to have better tests of her claims here.

Finally, the Jamesian point about pretensions suggests that high self-esteem may be more difficult to sustain than low self-esteem. Presumably, there are some people who are good at so few things that they risk running out of options on which to hang their claims to high self-worth. It is more difficult to imagine that anyone could run out of things to think themselves bad at. Despite this, very high self-esteem is far more common than very low self-esteem (Baumeister *et al.*, 1989).

Rejections and acceptances

Another possible source of esteem to have been studied in some detail relates to people's experience of the labour market. In a sense, this represents another domain of successes and failures, though the judgement of an intermediary is more obviously involved. An employer accepts the application for employment or rejects it, continues the employment or terminates it.

The evidence is quite consistent here too. Losing one's job, failing to find work and spending time unemployed are all associated with lower self-esteem. Moreover, these experiences appear to produce the differences in self-esteem rather than being produced by them (but recall that childhood self-esteem does affect the chances of experiencing longer periods of unemployment in adulthood, cf. Feinstein, 2000).

Several studies compare the self-esteem of employed and unemployed adults and report that the latter score lower on measures of self-esteem (e.g. Muller *et al.*, 1993). But this evidence leaves the causal direction of influence unresolved. More informative evidence comes from longitudinal studies. A number of researchers have taken advantage of the data available from the US National Longitudinal Study of Youth. This included information about the self-esteem of young people during their high school education and about post-education employment history.

Using these data, Goldsmith *et al.* (1996, 1997), Dooley and Prause (1995) and Prause and Dooley (1997) were able to determine that experience of both unemployment and unsatisfactory employment was associated with lower self-esteem, and that the size of the effects was related to the length of these experiences. Dooley and Prause, taking into account earlier self-esteem, could refine the nature of the impact. In the sample as a whole, self-esteem actually increased over a seven-year period, but increased significantly less for those who had the more negative employment experiences.

However, as with educational attainment, the effects found are generally small. Goldsmith *et al.* (1997) described one of the main effects as equivalent to a blemish. Many of the same options are available here either to discount misfortune in the labour market or to discount good fortune. And some new ones are available. The human agent – the employer – can be blamed and/or general economic conditions can be held responsible.

Though unemployment undoubtedly is linked to loss of esteem, even if the link is attenuated by various kinds of denial, it is not necessarily direct. Unemployment can have a number of consequences each of which may themselves have a direct impact on esteem. Among these are social isolation and loss of social support, economic stresses and loss of routine.

Finally, we have already seen that a range of public attacks on a person's worth – being diagnosed an alcoholic or convicted of child abuse, for example – can lower self-esteem. Some of the standard defensive tactics may be less effective against these assaults.

Zimmerman *et al.*'s (1997) finding that in a sample of around 1,100 young people a group could be identified whose self-esteem fell steadily from age 12 to 16 is open to a similar interpretation. This group also increased their misuse of alcohol more than others and their academic performance declined more. It may be that a personal sense of failure – loss of self-control through addiction to drugs or, as perhaps in this case, through frequent inebriation – damages self-esteem. It may also, however, be damaged by the very public nature of the failures. On the other hand, in the cases of delinquency, drug use and to some extent academic failure, the impact of public disapproval will be offset by choosing as friends other young people in the same position.

Appearance

One factor young people consistently mention when asked what particularly affects the way they feel about themselves is their physical appearance. Furthermore, the correlations between self-esteem and perceptions of physical appearance are high, and exceptionally so in adolescence. Harter (1998) reports correlations from her own research with teenagers in the range 0.65 to 0.82. At the upper end, this is close to the theoretical maximum. It would mean that self-esteem in some groups of young people, therefore, is entirely dependent on physical appearance.

Here, at last, in physical attributes, is a form of difference between people that is highly obvious, conspicuous and undeniable. Additionally, whatever comforting myths may say about beauty and the eye of the beholder, shared standards for attractiveness do exist. To be beautiful or handsome, to have the ideal body shape is to be desirable and desired. To differ from these ideals is to be less desirable, in direct proportion to the disparity. Is it not therefore to be expected that physical appearance will have a powerful influence on self-esteem?

It may be a reasonable expectation, particularly given this compelling evidence, but for one thing. The evidence concerns self-perceptions of physical appearance, not actual physical appearance. The relation between the two, or rather the relation between self-evaluated appearance and evaluations made by uninvolved observers (i.e. not family members or friends) is only moderate. And it is clear that the self-esteem is related to the self-evaluation, not to the objective reality. So, it is still to be explained why people believe what they do about their own appearance. The larger part of what they believe is not determined by the reality.

Similar things have been found with respect to body shape and body weight. Beliefs are imperfectly aligned with reality. One recent study nicely illustrates the consequences. Kostanski and Gullone (1998) found that body mass index (a measure of the appropriateness of weight given height) was related to dissatisfaction with body weight, but not perfectly related. Self-esteem was also related to dissatisfaction, but again imperfectly related. At the same time, self-esteem was quite unrelated to the body mass index. What this strongly suggests is that satisfaction with one's body is partly influenced by its objective proportions. But it is also and quite independently influenced by self-esteem.

In the cases of shape and weight, however, the ideals are culturally rather than medically determined. And this relates to the slightly lower average self-esteem of females noted above and most marked towards the end of adolescence, 15 to 18 years. An ideal in our culture at variance with the average has been particularly salient for women – much more exaggerated slimness than is typical. It is noteworthy that one of the few reasonably clear effects of low self-esteem is on eating disorders and that these disorders are far more prevalent among women.

Factors that have a substantial effect: (the behaviour of) parents

To the question, 'what are the most important influences on self-esteem?', the simple answer is parents. Cooley (1902) and then Mead (1934) anticipated that the self-concept would be shaped by the appraisals of significant others. More precisely, Cooley thought that the appraisals *anticipated* would matter, and Mead similarly discussed seeing ourselves as we *imagine* others see us. But, as psychologists were to point out later, we do not have to imagine what our parents think of us. Their views will be difficult to avoid while we remain with them.

What is more, throughout childhood at least, no other people will assume so much emotional significance for us. Our parents' views will matter and they will matter rather a lot.

Coopersmith (1967) was one of the first to emphasise the key role of parents in the development of self-esteem. He concluded that four qualities of their behaviour towards their children would be crucial. These were:

- the amount of acceptance, approval and affection shown

- the degree to which clear standards of behaviour were promoted and expected

- the degree to which discipline and control were based on explanation rather than force or coercion

- the extent to which they invited their children to express views about family decisions, in effect valuing the child as a contributor.

Subsequent research has supported these conclusions. It has also indicated that some of these qualities play a larger part than others. A recent review of this evidence (Feiring and Taska, 1996) singles out approval and acceptance. There are also indications (e.g. Richards *et al.*, 1991) that the support of mothers is more important to sons whereas the support of fathers is more important to daughters, a surprising endorsement of Freudian theory.

It is as yet less clear whether this remains true into adolescence. Some recent British research points to the key role of paternal support and interest in sustaining the self-esteem of sons as they move through adolescence (Katz, 2000). Rosenberg (1979) anticipated that parental influence on self-esteem would decline across adolescence, to be replaced in importance by the approval and acceptance of peers. Other research only partly supports this prediction. Self-esteem does become more aligned with peer approval but parents' opinions remain significant well into the adolescent and even adult years (e.g. Kashubeck and Christensen, 1995; van Aken and Asendorpf, 1997; Welsh and Stewart, 1995).

Quality of communication between parents and their children also regularly emerges as linked to levels of self-esteem. This may be, however, because the effort by parents to communicate well signals the degree to which they value the child.

Given the manifest importance of the quality of parental involvement, it will come as no surprise that parental abuse should have a devastating effect on self-esteem. Study after study shows that experiencing physical abuse in childhood at the hands of one's parents or guardians causes significant and lasting damage to self-esteem. The effects of sexual abuse are if anything even more damaging.

One review of research on child sexual abuse (Browne and Finkelor, 1986) singled out low self-esteem as one of the more conspicuous long-term effects. In one of the reviewed studies, victims of this abuse were four times more likely than others to be the lowest scorers on a self-esteem measure. The reviewers also concluded that the damage is greater to the extent that a father figure was involved, genital contact was involved and force was involved. A more recent review (Kendall-Tackett *et al.*, 1993) for which rather more evidence was by then available – 45 studies – came to almost identical conclusions. Similar effects of abuse could be expected from anyone else acting *in loco parentis* during childhood or early adolescence.

Another unsurprising source of low self-esteem is family breakdown (e.g. Armistead *et al.*, 1995). Precisely how this effect occurs, however, is not clear. The damage could be done by the conflict between parents leading to the breakdown. Alternatively, the damage could be done by the apparent lack of parental concern for the child signalled by the breakdown, or by the loss of social support that results from the breakdown.

Similarly, the documented association between homelessness and low self-esteem is difficult to untangle from those of conditions that resulted in homelessness. But the state of homelessness can have its own, magnifying effects, for example through social isolation, lack of social support or the daily experience of rejection.

Do other kinds of victimisation – being bullied at school or work, harassed or verbally abused in public because, for example, one is homeless, being assaulted or abused by a partner or spouse, being raped – damage self-esteem? All these kinds of victimisation are associated with lower self-esteem. For example, a recent meta-analysis confirmed this very clearly for victimisation by peers (Hawker and Boulton, 2000). But there is a complication. Some recent work shows that the probability of being victimised in at least some of these ways is higher for children and adults whose self-esteem is already low (e.g. Egan and Perry, 1998). In another recent longitudinal study (Horowitz, 1999), low self-esteem predicted risk of subsequently being a victim of domestic violence. This being so, it is not clear what the earlier evidence of an association between low self-esteem and victimisation actually means. This is one area that would certainly benefit from further research.

Genes

There is one significant respect in which biological parents may influence the self-esteem of their children, namely through the genes. Thus far, there are few studies of the scale of genetic influences on variations in self-esteem, so any conclusions for the present must be tentative. Perhaps the most useful piece of evidence on this point to date comes from a study of 3,793 twin pairs in America (Kendler *et al.*, 1998). Both twins in each of these pairs – the age range was 18 to 60 years – completed the Rosenberg measure of self-esteem. Heritability estimates were similar for both sexes; just under one-third of the variation in self-esteem scores could be attributed to inherited differences in the sample. This would make the genes, by a large margin, the single most important source of variations in self-esteem.

Knowing this is important for at least two reasons. First, it indicates that self-esteem can independently influence such outcomes as suicide attempts, eating disorders, or teenage pregnancy. In other words, in respect of these kinds of outcome, it is not necessarily a mediator of the effects of other circumstances such as experience of physical abuse in childhood.

Second, it means that most of the differences between people in their self-esteem – though it will be less than 70 per cent because some allowance must be made for measurement error – is produced by the different things that happen to people in the course of their lives, that is to say by variations in experience or circumstances. So, in principle at least, self-esteem is amenable to change through planned intervention, i.e. by changing experiences and circumstances. This is also strongly suggested by the no more than moderate stability of self-esteem test scores over time.

The relative immunity of established self-esteem: are there any other significant others?

After parents and beyond mid-adolescence, no one else seems to achieve the same level of influence over self-esteem. In this respect, the expectations of symbolic interactionists have not been borne out. Their key prediction was that opinions of the self would be based on the anticipated reactions of others, or on what were referred to as 'reflected appraisals'. It seems that the actual reactions of others may have very little influence on what we think of ourselves. It is almost as if, after our parents have had their say – and their genetic influence – we become increasingly deaf to other, especially dissenting, voices.

The range of tactics for coping with failures that contradict self-evaluations (or successes if those self-evaluations are low) turn out to have more general application. Feedback from others that contradicts self-evaluations is similarly discounted.

These defensive patterns bear on the question of whether self-esteem is primarily affective (in which case judgements are driven by feelings) or cognitive (in which case feelings are driven by judgements).

If judgement – a cognitive process – was primary, one might expect it to be progressively adjusted to reality so that eventually (e.g. by adulthood) the fit would be pretty good. In other words, children's judgements about themselves may not be very accurate. But the progressive accumulation of experience combined with growing ability to make accurate judgements should in the longer term result in judgements about the self that would concur with those of a detached observer. The fact that this is just not the case – that people's views of themselves are only weakly related to any independent assessment of their relative worth or standing – indicates the primacy of feelings. It suggests the way we feel about ourselves in general terms strongly biases the judgements we make about our various qualities and attributes, and likewise biases the way we treat feedback from others about these qualities.

It also needs to be emphasised here that very few people have low self-esteem in an absolute sense – in that they more often describe themselves in negative than in positive terms. Baumeister and his colleagues have shown in a careful analysis of the ways in which responses to self-esteem measures are distributed that the average position is moderately positive, indeed on the high side of moderately positive (Baumeister *et al.*, 1989). Therefore, the references in research to low versus high self-esteem almost always mean a distinction between those whose self-esteem is very positive and those whose self-esteem is slightly positive.

The very positives are likely to have an unrealistic view of themselves. And, among other things, their unrealistic optimism leads them to take risks. They are more likely to believe (unrealistically) that they will not suffer negative consequences in doing so. This would, for example, entail unrealistic optimism about the risks of drug abuse, smoking, excessive alcohol consumption, getting caught for crimes, or engaging in a range of physically hazardous pursuits (like driving fast). They also effectively take risks in the claims they make about their own worth.

Those below the average in self-esteem – which means slightly positive – are more realistic, more cautious and also pessimistic. Their behavioural strategies seem to be based on self-protection rather than self-promotion. They don't want to run the risk of failure or having their claims discredited, so they predict failure.

To return to the question of significant others, our relationships with others may affect our self-esteem not just because we care whether they applaud our successes or criticise our failures. It may be as important and perhaps more important that we are accepted, liked and loved. Recall the evidence that a key quality of parent–child relations is acceptance. Recall also Leary's proposal that self-esteem is a form of barometer, reflecting the degree to which we are included or excluded by others. So, do peers, partners, friends, spouses become significant others as we move into adolescence and adulthood for these kinds of reasons?

Unfortunately, research evidence to date is not entirely clear on this question. One reason is the now familiar problem of deciding what is cause and what is effect. There are moreover entirely good reasons to expect that self-esteem will have an effect on relationships. A second reason is the sheer number of aspects of relationships with others that could in principle be relevant. Is it, for example, important to be popular with many people or to be liked by a few? Does it matter who likes you and who does not? Does the degree of intimacy in key relationships matter? A third reason is that the researcher's source of information about aspects and qualities of relationships is often the same as that about self-esteem. That is to say the researcher compares people's self-esteem with their own *perceptions* of their relationships with others.

Bearing in mind these difficulties, what does the evidence show? First, self-esteem is clearly related to perceptions of various aspects of relationships with others. For instance, both Vaux (1988) and McWhirter (1997) found that low self-esteem was associated with feelings of loneliness. However, evidence reported by Olmstead *et al.* (1991) indicates that this could be an effect of self-esteem rather than one of social or emotional isolation. They found that self-esteem in adolescence predicted loneliness ten years later.

Turning to more specific qualities of relationships, findings are mixed but the majority indicate some connection with self-esteem. The study by Field *et al.* (1995) of 455 teenagers showed that self-esteem was related to perceived level of intimacy with parents but not especially with a best friend. In contrast, Franco and Levitt's (1998) study of a younger group, ten to 11 year olds, did reveal a clear association between self-esteem and perceived friendship quality. But their data also raise the possibility that both self-esteem and perceived friendship quality may be consequences of the quality of their relationships with their parents. Wiltfang and Scarbecz (1990) found that adolescents' perceptions of the number of friends they had and the degree to which they occupied a leadership position in the peer group were related, if weakly, to self-esteem.

On the basis of her own review of the evidence, Harter (1998) concludes that, in adolescence at least, friendship is of less consequence than indications of social standing within the wider peer group. But not all the evidence points unambiguously in this direction. For example, Townsend *et al.* (1988) found that, for a sample of 13 to 15 year olds, their self-esteem was more closely related to their perceptions of the intimacy of their friendships than to their popularity. Popularity may also be less of an issue in adulthood.

Self-esteem appears to be correlated with various indicators of marital satisfaction and harmony, though only moderately (e.g. Lee and Shelan, 1989; Shackelford, 2001; Voss *et al.*, 1999). More specifically, Ferroni and Taft (1997) found in a study of 656 Australian women aged between 30 and 50 that higher self-esteem went with better communication with their partners.

It may be a mistake, however, to focus exclusively on marriage. People are typically embedded in a network of relationships. The potential importance of this is indicated by various studies including Winefield *et al.*'s (1992) survey of 483 adults. This revealed a clear link between self-esteem and perceived social support. A series of studies of adult women by Brown and his colleagues (e.g. Brown *et al.*, 1990) pointed to quite strong associations between their self-esteem and the negative and positive qualities of their close relationships. Lee and Shelan (1989) found that extent of association with friends was related to self-esteem in older age. Finally, Leary's attempts to test his barometer interpretation of self-esteem deserve a mention here. He and his colleagues found, in a sample of college students, that self-esteem was quite strongly associated with perceived degree of inclusion and acceptance by others (Leary *et al.*, 1995).

Each of the above studies relies on relating individuals' self-esteem to their own perceptions of their relationships with others. Their conclusions are therefore vulnerable to the possibility that self-esteem itself distorts the relevant perceptions. Thus, high self-esteem may produce unrealistically positive views of relations with others while low self-esteem may have the opposite effect. Significantly, Borhnstedt and Felson (1983) found that judgements about matters that tend to be rather ambiguous, like one's personal popularity, are influenced by one's self-esteem rather than the reverse.

Independent evidence about relationships would be desirable for these reasons, and a few studies do provide such evidence. With respect to adolescence, Bishop and Inderbitzen (1995) found that self-esteem was unrelated to *actual* popularity or to the sheer number of friends. But it was higher among those with at least one reciprocated friendship. Keefe and Berndt (1996) found that adolescents who had stable friendships also had higher self-esteem, though this stability was no more likely than its absence to lead to any subsequent increase in self-esteem. Stanley and Arora's (1998) study of 101 teenage girls indicated that those who were frequently excluded from friendship groups had lower self-esteem. Finally, Emler *et al.* (2000) found a modest relation between the self-esteem of young adults and others' judgements of the intimacy of their relationships with these individuals.

Though these studies confirm that links between self-esteem and qualities of relationships are not entirely illusory, the question of causal direction remains. Longitudinal evidence is of more help here, but to date there is still very little of it. One ten-year study, by Giordano *et al.* (1998), suggests no link at all between the quality of close relationships and later self-esteem. This is what they found when comparing the intimacy of adolescent friendships with the self-esteem of 620 of their sample ten years on and into early adulthood.

The picture is different in other studies, however. Aron and colleagues (1995) followed up a group of 529 undergraduates over a much shorter period and found that self-esteem went up after falling in love. Cramer has also studied this population over short periods and has found clear evidence of a causal influence running from relationship quality to self-esteem (e.g. Cramer, 1990). One of the qualities that appears to be crucial is unconditional acceptance by a close friend. Andrews and Brown (1995) made a special study of 102 adult women initially identified as having low self-esteem. This group was followed up over

seven years and positive changes in self-esteem appeared to be linked to improvements in relationship quality. It may be, therefore, that our self-esteem is more dependent on the current quality of our relationships with others than it is upon how close we may have been to other people in the past.

When it comes to self-esteem, in the long run, parents are not the only significant others in our lives, even though they may remain pre-eminent. But the influence in the other direction – of self-esteem on relationships – also needs to be taken seriously. People with high self-esteem, as we have already seen, pay little attention to adverse feedback, and this is also true of relationship-relevant feedback (Emler *et al.*, 2000; Nezlek *et al.*, 1997).

Though this may at first sight appear to be a disadvantage, it could help to overcome the conflicts and low points that are features of almost all relationships. People with high self-esteem appear to have better social skills (Riggio *et al.*, 1990), and to have more of the social competencies relevant to forming and developing close relationships (Burhmester *et al.*, 1988). They also perceive conflicts in their relationships as less serious and their friendships as more robust (Azmitia *et al.*, 1999). They seem to have better options for coping with conflict when it arises in their relationships (Schuetz, 1998). They are more confident that friendly overtures will be reciprocated (Baldwin and Keelan, 1999), that the people they like will like them (Wiest, 1965). And they disclose more about themselves to others (Dolgin *et al.*, 1991), an inclination that has been found to be important in forming and developing close ties with others.

All in all, people with high self-esteem seem to have a number of inclinations that together with their generally more optimistic demeanour should be assets in forming, developing and sustaining successful close relationships. There are indications to this effect earlier in life. For example, Hart and his colleagues (Hart *et al.*, 1997) found that a group of Icelandic children, distinguished from their peers at age seven in being more overcontrolled, had lower self-esteem and were more socially withdrawn in adolescence. Similarly, Fordham and Hinde (1999), following a small sample of children from five to ten years, found that self-esteem related to observed shyness as well as to several aspects of their relations with peers. Another longitudinal study, this time of adolescents (Armistead *et al.*, 1995), indicated that self-esteem predicted the quality of peer relations six years on.

Finally, there is a question about the effects of social exclusion – in the sense of limited personal contacts. Employment status has a dramatic effect on the social contacts of young people. Those who leave school and either fail to find work or to go into further training have substantially less regular contact with many fewer people than their peers of the same age who stay in full-time education, enter employment or embark upon further education (Emler, 2000). Given other evidence for a link between social support and self-esteem (e.g. Winefield *et al.*, 1992), this raises a question about the possible effects of such impoverishment of social life upon the self-esteem of young people. As yet, we do not have the evidence to answer this question.

Conclusions: the sources of self-esteem

The largest single source of variations in self-esteem is genetic. It now seems that at least one-third of the variation may be attributable to this one factor. Next in importance come the various things that parents do to their children. But these effects do not end with childhood; parents continue to be potent influences into adolescence and beyond. Other close relationships may in the longer run assume considerable importance but the very existence and success of such relationships are quite probably also effects of self-esteem, and thus indirectly of parental influences.

Next, there are various circumstances, experiences and conditions that have some effect on self-esteem, but not effects of the same order. Real successes and failures do matter, but not so much as perceptions of these. How well one does in one's career has effects on self-esteem but here, too, perceived and actual accomplishments are not the same thing. Appearance also matters, but not remotely so much as beliefs about appearance. It is clear that self-esteem is not simply the sum of the judgements one makes about oneself. It shapes those judgements. Self-esteem profoundly affects the ways in which evidence about the self is interpreted.

This is apparent with respect to some of the factors that have little or no discernible impact on self-esteem. Whether one is male or female does have an effect, and several explanations have been advanced as to why this might be so. But the effect is small and these explanations predict far more difference than has ever been shown. It has, for example, been suggested that the relative social prestige of the categories of male and female is an influence here. But it does not seem to be an influence with respect to ethnicity or social class.

Knowing something about the normal influences on self-esteem, about the nature of self-esteem and about the sources of resistance to change in self-esteem now puts us in a better position to consider the prospects for interventions intended to raise self-esteem.

4 Changing self-esteem: the effectiveness of planned interventions

This chapter can be relatively short. It would be short if self-esteem were impossible to modify, or if such change had rarely been attempted. But neither of these are true. However, brevity is also appropriate when there is little relevant to be said, as is the case here. The reality is that there are still very few firm conclusions about what works in planned interventions or why.

Ignorance in these respects has clearly been no impediment to confidence in the possibility of raising self-esteem. Much of the popular literature on self-esteem is sold on the promise of raising self-esteem, either one's own, one's partner's or one's children's. And, beyond the self-help manuals, a vast army of therapists, social workers, educators, youth workers and other professionals is engaged in delivering programmes intended to improve the self-esteem of those who receive them. The impression is that for many of those involved the enterprise is more than a service, or even an industry, it is a noble and righteous crusade.

One programme, POPS (the Power of Positive Students), which has been disseminated to several thousand schools in the United States, has been promoted on the claim that 'the key to performance and behavior is self-esteem' (POPS International Foundation, 1994, p. 2). The expectations of its promoters are hardly modest: 'eighty-eight to ninety-two percent of success is due to attitude' (Weisman, 1991, p. 17), a curiously precise if wildly inflated estimate. But this is also proselytising language. It is not a dispassionate, let alone a disinterested, appraisal of the merits of the enterprise.

A problem with crusades and to some extent with industries is that the vested interests of those involved are at odds with critical evaluation. If you are selling a product – and rewarded materially or otherwise for doing so successfully – you have a strong interest in believing that it works. This inevitably favours one of two responses to

evaluation, to interpret the evidence optimistically or not to take the risk of collecting any in the first place. It should therefore come as no surprise that the level of effort invested in developing and running programmes to raise self-esteem has not been remotely matched by efforts to evaluate these programmes. But what we really need to know is whether they work.

In fact there are several things we need to know:

- Do the programmes work at all?

- How well do they work (how substantial and enduring are the changes produced)?

- With which target groups do they work best?

- How efficient are they (what is the relation between the gains achieved and the costs involved)?

- Why do they work?

This last is practically relevant for two related reasons. First, many programmes will contain a number of diverse elements. If they are not all relevant then the cost of the programme could be reduced and, in principle, offered more widely. Second, a clear understanding as to why an intervention works should allow us to devise more efficient and effective programmes. As we shall see, however, at present there is little basis for decisively answering any of these questions except perhaps for the first. There are the beginnings of answers to the second and last questions, but they are so far only the sketchiest of answers.

Before considering these answers, the options for raising self-esteem merit a brief look. There are three sources of ideas about how self-esteem could be raised through deliberate intervention, namely theory, the research evidence on the determinants of self-esteem (reviewed in the previous chapter), and the methods that have in practice been developed and tried.

How self-esteem might be raised: theory as a source of ideas

A sensible place to start is with a theory of the phenomenon and then to follow through its implications for changing self-esteem. The Jamesian successes/pretensions formula contains two clear implications for such change. The first is to alter the level of success a person enjoys. This may not appear to be very practical but this option is not to be dismissed out of hand. Programmes that concentrate on developing skills of various kinds could, through their impact on performance, produce improvements in self-esteem.

Nevertheless, the second implication looks more promising: modify aspirations. In principle at least, it should be easier to modify people's goals than the abilities they need to achieve these goals. Two kinds of option can be distinguished here. One is to alter the relative importance of different goals. The related message here may be that we need to change public attitudes about the kinds of accomplishment that are valued and move away, particularly in secondary education, from privileging one form of success – narrowly defined academic – over all others (cf. Robinson *et al.*'s [1990] observations on the relative merits of English and French secondary education). The other option is to change the level of particular goals, in effect to move goals to more realistic and achievable levels.

The implication of Cooley's 'looking-glass self' is perhaps that self-esteem can be improved by altering patterns of association: avoid exposure to conspicuously talented, successful or attractive people. The reach and content of contemporary mass media clearly make this very difficult for young people. Accomplished and beautiful people are massively over-represented in magazines, television and film. But, if this is a problem, it may also have a solution, namely education in the interpretation of these media (cf. Kusel, 1999).

From Rosenberg's interpretation of self-esteem as an attitude, we could take the message that

attention should be given to the optimal conditions for attitude change. Contemporary research into the nature of these conditions tells us the following (cf. Eagly and Chaiken, 1993; Petty and Wegener, 1998): a large number of conditions affect the likelihood of attitude change but among these the quality of arguments can actually be very important; the impact of good arguments itself depends on a variety of conditions.

When an issue is important to people, when they are highly involved, they are more inclined to put effort into examining the arguments intended to change their views. Under these circumstances, the quality of the arguments becomes particularly relevant; people are more persuaded by good arguments than by poor ones. Insofar as the self is an important issue, then one's self-esteem is more likely to be changed when one is presented with good arguments for doing so. This common-sense view seems almost too straightforward to be true. What makes it less straightforward is the number of circumstances that can undermine the impact of good arguments.

Rudimentary requirements are that the arguments actually be noticed and then be understood. People can fail to understand because an argument is garbled, confused, or not clearly expressed. An elementary if often neglected requirement therefore is that arguments are presented in a straightforward manner that can be readily understood by those for whom they are intended. People may also fail to notice the argument because too many other things are simultaneously competing for their attention. On the whole it is easier to capture and hold the attention of small groups than large groups.

Recall also that people with low self-esteem are less readily persuaded than those whose self-esteem is moderate (see Chapter 2, section on 'Health risks and susceptibility to influence'). This seems to be because they fail to detect attempts at persuasion. Thus, programmes aimed at raising low self-esteem do need to give special attention to these basic requirements. And there is probably still much that could be learned in this respect from the research literature on attitude change. Among the techniques that might be borrowed is 'counter-attitudinal role-playing', a process shown to be capable of producing enduring changes in attitudes. This involves acting out or rehearsing the arguments for a position that is contrary to one's own initial views.

Finally under the heading of theory, the so-called hierarchical model deserves mention. This model interprets self-esteem as the sum of specific evaluations of oneself in different domains. It is the model underlying 'aggregate' measures of self-esteem. Its implication is that self-esteem is most likely to be changed by altering each of the elements that contribute to it. For example, an intervention might seek to change individuals' perceptions and evaluations of their appearance, their level of competence and success in various domains, their standing with peers, classmates, teachers, family and so on. A further implication is that individuals will differ in the areas of their self-perceived weaknesses so that the impact of a single intervention will vary from one individual to another. Its effectiveness will vary as a function of its 'fit' with the particular weaknesses of each individual who participates.

How self-esteem might be raised: research evidence as a source of ideas

The most obvious message from evidence of the determinants of self-esteem for programmes intended to raise low self-esteem, particularly in childhood and early adolescence, is: change the behaviour of the parents. Many programmes seek to do just this. The research also tells us *what* to try and change in their behaviour. Acceptance and approval, together with practices that convey these – making time for their children, paying attention, taking an interest, listening, encouraging initiative, being fair, having clear and positive expectations –

seem to be key. But there are also practical limits to what can be done with parents, limits that include their own willingness to change. Moreover, when self-esteem has been damaged by family breakdown, the limits may be insurmountable.

For these reasons, we need to consider the other significant influences on self-esteem. Insofar as close friendships are valuable, then interventions that enhance ability to form and hold on to these relationships could be expected to benefit self-esteem. We have also seen that physical appearance together with real successes and failures has some impact on self-esteem. But we have seen as well that perceptions are consistently more important than the realities. It does not follow that there is no point in trying to change the realities and there may be some, albeit limited, scope for doing so. Thus, theory favouring interventions that increase skills and competencies is also consistent with the evidence.

It does follow, however, that attempting to change perceptions can be more profitable, not to mention cheaper. This brings us back to attitude change. But the options depend on the existing discrepancies between perceptions and realities. Some children who are by any objective test well above the average in academic ability or attainment also have low self-esteem. Their self-esteem could be raised by altering the perception to match the reality. But this is hardly an option for those other children who have equally low self-esteem but also below average academic attainment.

Generally, a focus on aligning perceptions with real successes, real talents, real assets is a risky strategy, given that there are genuine differences in these or else social rankings deeply rooted in the culture. Covington (1989), who reviewed the links between low self-esteem and failure in school for the California Task Force, wished to indict the culture of achievement. Ranking, he argued, was built into the system; it created failure. The Task Force was unwilling to go this far and effectively ignored his conclusions (Kahne, 1996). Intervention to change people's beliefs about themselves is one thing. Changing cultural belief systems and entire socio-economic structures is quite another. There is therefore a considerable advantage to be had from the fact that self-esteem is not naturally tied so very closely to real successes and failures, real talents or liabilities.

The hope that everyone may turn out to have at least one significant talent on which to hang some self-esteem is ultimately equally risky. A more realisable approach might be to encourage each individual to use themselves as their own benchmark. We are back with James's point about adjusting pretensions or, in the modern parlance, setting achievable personal goals. In other words, rather than emphasising a common standard against which some will inevitably perform better than others, individuals could be led to pursue realistic goals based on their own current levels of achievement.

A final point that might be taken from the evidence about self-esteem is to notice how it is normally defended. Low self-esteem, like high self-esteem, seems to be sustained by a variety of defences – selective attention, biased evaluation of confirming and disconfirming evidence, biased attributions of successes and failures, selective memory and so on. This suggests that interventions should directly attack the various defences.

How self-esteem might be raised: varieties of intervention in practice

The practice arena abounds with acronyms. More or less widely tried if not tested programmes include KICK, DARE, GREAT, SMILE, GOAL (and POP) among others, as well as suggestively named interventions like Little Acorns and Big Buddies, each with an implicit if not explicit theory as to what damages or depresses self-esteem and what can raise it. Indeed, there are so many of these that in the United States there is a National Council for Self-esteem providing details on the range of

curricula available. There are also by a long way too many to describe here.

The variety is immense. Some programmes focus on providing particular kinds of information, others on developing competencies, or training particular patterns of behaviour or modifying existing habits of behaviour, yet others on modifying attitudes or perceptions. Many are eclectic packages of measures. There are also immense variations in forms of delivery – individual therapy, self-help, physical exercises, group-based, peer-tutoring, whole family – in intensity and in length. The following is intended as illustrative of the range and variety.

Pope and his colleagues (1988) have developed a programme specifically for children and adolescents and based upon the Jamesian idea that low self-esteem results from a discrepancy between aspirations and achievements. The programme is intended to change both. It seeks to change the former by modifying the standards the child aspires to, the latter by training skills to enable greater achievements. It makes use of well-established principles of learning to produce these changes. To be more specific, it relies on demonstrations of actions or arguments by a teacher that the participants are then encouraged to imitate and practice, and their efforts are then rewarded through approval and praise (positive reinforcements) from the teacher.

The approach assumes that self-esteem is shaped by achievements in different domains – school, social life, family, body – and the programme proceeds from diagnosis of each individual's profile of self-esteem needs. A separate module of the programme is devoted to each domain. Within each module, eight skill areas are addressed in turn: learning to solve social problems, developing positive self-statements, using a realistic attributional style, improving self-control, setting appropriate standards, developing social understanding and skills, enhancing communication skills, improving body image.

The programme as a whole is strongly oriented to skill acquisition. It emphasises rehearsal and practice so that performance becomes increasingly habitual and automatic. It also emphasises generalisation of new habits; participants are encouraged to apply these skills to their lives outside the programme. Although the programme is promoted as 'individualised' – shaped to the particular needs of each individual – it is also claimed that it can be delivered to groups, typically in one or two 30- to 60-minute sessions per week. 'Homework' between sessions provides some of its individualised character while regular and frequent sessions are necessary to ensure that feedback will help consolidate learning.

In contrast, Bednar *et al.* (1989) have developed a system that is much closer to traditional psychotherapy. It is based on one-to-one sessions with a highly trained and experienced clinician. It is intensive and long-term, and therefore requires considerable commitment on the part of the patient. It is also therefore a very expensive solution.

Mruk (1999), discussing these and some of the other better-established programmes, suggests they indicate that there are several effective techniques to enhance self-esteem. Improving problem-solving skills is just one of these. Also on his list are: being accepting and caring; providing consistent affirming feedback (emphasising the positive); cognitive restructuring (essentially changing attitudes and perceptions); assertiveness training (empowerment); modelling (showing by doing – for example, demonstrating a more effective method for handling conflict; the Pope *et al.* [1988] programme does actually include this as a teaching tool); using 'natural self-esteem moments'.

This last refers to the observations (e.g. Epstein, 1979) that self-esteem does change spontaneously in response to various events, particularly to transitions in life, and that interventions can exploit these to magnify their potential positive effects.

Most programmes use some combination of these techniques. But do they actually work?

Does anything work at all?

Given the discussion in the previous chapter of the range of conditions which seem to have little or no effect on self-esteem and of the range of defences with which an established level of self-esteem is sustained, we should not expect it to be easily changed. However, total pessimism would be inappropriate. Epstein's interest in 'natural self-esteem moments' concerned events in adulthood that seemed capable of moving self-esteem in either direction. But there is also clear evidence of change at various transition points in adolescence. For example, the move from primary to secondary appears to produce a downward change. This effect is also greater and more long-lasting if the move occurs early. The timing of puberty likewise has an effect – early maturing girls, for example, are at a disadvantage.

On the positive side, self-esteem does increase over the course of adolescence. Hart *et al.* (1993) suggest this because young people become increasingly adept at remaking themselves, shedding less desirable attributes and habits. There is also a clear upward movement at the end of secondary education (e.g. Schulenberg *et al.*, 2000). Self-esteem change in a positive direction clearly is possible beyond the end of childhood. But the question is: can deliberate interventions produce positive changes?

There are certain general requirements for ideal outcome evaluation and these apply equally to the evaluation of self-esteem enhancement programmes. The most basic of these is the inclusion of an appropriate control group. Some evaluations are limited to comparing self-esteem at the start and completion of the programme. Given that the programme may last a considerable time – a year is not uncommon – and may also span some significant transition points, spontaneous gains are entirely possible. One has to show that any improvement over the course of the programme is greater than any change in this direction that would have occurred anyway.

It is also desirable that the control group have something equivalent to a placebo. Positive change can result from incidental features of interventions, for example the fact of being singled out and given special attention.

A third requirement is that inclusion in the intervention rather than the control group should be entirely random. Interventions frequently rely on volunteers. Non-volunteers may differ from volunteers in crucial respects. If the control group consists of young people who did not volunteer or whose parents were unwilling for them to be included in the programme, then both differences and lack of differences become difficult to interpret.

The literature on evaluation is limited, but it is growing all the time. There have also been some reviews of this literature. The most recent and most useful review to date is Haney and Durlak's (1998) meta-analysis of 116 studies, though it only covers studies published before 1992. Haney and Durlak point out that many interventions have assessed self-esteem as an outcome while having a different primary purpose, for example to improve social or learning skills. Their analysis includes relevant studies of these interventions. They were relevant if additionally the targeted groups were 18 years or younger, and if the evaluation included a control group drawn from the same population.

The programmes they review therefore included a wide range of methods and populations. They included well-established curricula such as DUSO (Developing Understanding of Self and Others), classroom-based programmes delivered by teachers, interventions involving relaxation techniques, training in social problem solving and interventions involving role-playing exercises.

Just over half of the studies reviewed involved prevention as opposed to treatment (for specific diagnosed problems). Just over half were of school-based programmes and the majority were delivered to groups rather than on a one-to-one basis. The mean length of a programme was around 20 weeks

with an average of 16 sessions, though the range for both was considerable – from two weeks to three years and from one to 95 sessions. The majority were targeted at the six to 12 year age range. Just under a quarter of the programmes had employed commercially produced curricula. Most of the evaluations of self-esteem effects were based on established and published scales, such as the Coopersmith inventory, the Rosenberg scale or the Piers-Harris scale. Because of the way in which many of the findings were reported, it was not possible for Haney and Durlak to examine the moderating effects of age or gender.

Over 60 per cent of the programmes did produce measurable positive change in self-esteem (though worryingly some 12.5 per cent actually produced clear negative changes). The mean effect size was modest. However, the size of the effects varied significantly with a number of factors.

Among these factors was whether the intervention was specifically intended to raise self-esteem or whether it had some other purpose and included self-esteem as an outcome measure. Interventions of the former kind were significantly and substantially more effective.

The design of the evaluation also made a difference. Designs involving randomised assignment to either the intervention programme or the control group showed larger effects of the intervention. What this indicates is that anything involving non-random assignment results in children being in the programme who are *less* likely to benefit from it (and correspondingly more of the children who would have been most likely to benefit from not being in it).

The type of control group was responsible for some additional differences in apparent effectiveness. If the control group simply involved no treatment of any kind, the difference between it and the programme was greater. This indicates that incidental features of interventions, such as singling children out for special attention and treatment, do have some effects additional to those features explicitly intended and expected to raise self-esteem.

Next Haney and Durlak established that the rationale for the intervention influenced its effectiveness, though it was only possible to reach quite general conclusions here. Interventions with a rationale based on prior research findings were the most successful. In other words, if research evidence had already shown that certain conditions reliably influence self-esteem, then an intervention which created these conditions was likely to be particularly successful. Next in effectiveness came interventions based on a clear theoretical justification, followed by interventions set up to test particular hypotheses. It is a reasonable guess that these latter were therefore derived from some theoretical view of self-esteem, even if more indirectly. Least successful were those without any clear rationale.

Finally, treatment interventions were substantially more effective than preventative interventions. This is not really surprising because interventions to treat particular problems associated with low self-esteem are almost by definition working with a segment of the population with the most scope for upward change. Unless prevention is focused on children at risk, initial levels of self-esteem should be average. As we have already seen, average self-esteem is likely to be high in absolute terms. The scope for further upward change is therefore necessarily more limited. Nonetheless, the impact of prevention programmes for self-esteem appears to be 'well within the range achieved by other primary prevention interventions' (Haney and Durlak, 1998, p. 429).

It is also worth mentioning features that had no discernible impact on effects. These included whether the programme was delivered to groups or individuals, the level of training or experience of those delivering the programme and its length.

Given that each of these has a significant impact on costs, these are important findings.

Given that the durability of effects is also highly important, it was unfortunate that so few of the programme evaluations – in fact only five – included any long-term follow-up. The average was a mere 16 weeks.

Haney and Durlak found that programmes did have effects on other outcomes, such as improvements in behaviours supposedly linked to self-esteem. Moreover, the scale of these effects was directly related to the scale of the effects on self-esteem. So, for example, a programme intended to raise self-esteem might also result in improved social skills or relations with peers, changes in eating patterns towards less harmful practices, or changes towards less risky sexual behaviour.

This is strongly suggestive, if for the moment no more than that, of the conclusion that self-esteem does indeed influence various forms of behaviour and performance. But it is still only suggestive. Equally possible is that the changes in behaviour or performance are responsible for the self-esteem changes, or that both are influenced by some other unmeasured change produced by the intervention. These questions require a better understanding as to why interventions work and what precisely are the crucial elements of those that do work.

Since 1992, there have been more evaluation studies. And the quality of evaluation methods has been improving. The consequences have not been uniformly positive except in the sense that we now have fewer excuses for wasted efforts. Some widely used programmes do not have the claimed effects on self-esteem. A notable example is DARE (Drug Abuse Resistance Education). This programme was developed for adolescents and designed to reduce drug use by raising self-esteem. It has been very widely used in the United States. And it has been the subject of several evaluations. The conclusions from these are clear and consistent. Its effects on self-esteem are either very limited or non-existent (e.g. Ennett *et al.*, 1994; Harmon, 1993; Lynam *et al.*, 2000). The Lynam *et al.* study provided a ten-year follow-up of impact on self-esteem. There was none. Sadly, it appears to have little impact on the target outcome either; it does not affect drug use.

Some of the other acronyms seem also to have promised more than they could deliver. For example, Gang Resistance Education And Training (GREAT) had, according to Palumbo and Ferguson (1995), no effect on self-esteem. The same story has emerged for the Big Buddies programme (Dennison, 2000), Rainbow for Children (Skitka and Frazier, 1995) and Project Charlie (Hurry and McGurk, 1997). Significantly, many of the failures are drug use/abuse prevention programmes (cf. also Stoil *et al.*, 2000). They are therefore focused on a problem to which the contribution of low self-esteem is at the very best questionable.

There are success stories and moreover successes which are confirmed by longer-term follow-ups. Moreover, the successes concern problems in which the case for an influence of low self-esteem looks clearer. These include a couple of interventions focused on eating problems. McFadden (1998) has reported self-esteem gains for NECTAR, a programme addressing food attitudes and behaviour. The gains, relative to a control group, were sustained at six- and 12-month follow-ups. A study by O'Dea and Abraham (2000), focusing on body image (see Appendix, section on 'Eating disorders'), showed improvements in both self-esteem and diet that were sustained one year after completion of the programme.

There is also accumulating evidence that some forms of psychotherapy work and have clear advantages over others in raising self-esteem. In particular, cognitive-behavioural therapies appear to be effective (e.g. Durham *et al.*, 1994). The term 'cognitive-behavioural' actually refers to a variety of different methods but what they have in common is an emphasis on changing the beliefs of the patient in conjunction with behaviour modification techniques. Given that these forms of

therapy have proved so effective in alleviating the symptoms of depression (e.g. Hollon and Garber, 1990), it is perhaps not surprising that they should also prove particularly effective when the outcome measure is self-esteem (e.g. Garner *et al.*, 1993). This is also consistent with Pelham and Swann's (1989) conclusions that the determinants of self-esteem are both affective (feelings) and cognitive (judgements or beliefs).

Rational emotive therapy (RET) (Ellis, 1973), although also regarded as a cognitive-behavioural technique, concentrates in particular upon altering maladaptive or irrational beliefs. It functions as a form of persuasion or attitude change, relying on rational arguments. Recall the earlier observations about self-esteem as an attitude and about the value in changing attitudes of strong arguments. Recall also the evidence that low self-esteem appears to entail irrational, inappropriate beliefs about the self. In the light of these, RET might appear a particularly appropriate technique for overcoming very low self-esteem. It does seem to produce improvements in self-esteem (e.g. Rieckert and Moeller, 2000), though it has not consistently been shown to be superior to other cognitive-behavioural techniques in this regard (Warren *et al.*, 1988).

The major disadvantage of these therapeutic techniques is their cost. As might be expected of techniques focused on changing attitudes and beliefs, they work well because they create conditions in which the patient is likely to attend to the message and to understand it (cf. the earlier comments about the importance of these conditions to attitude change). But these are typically conditions of one-to-one contact between patient and therapist. However, there are encouraging indications that, for example, rational emotive techniques can form the basis for group-based interventions (e.g. Leaf *et al.*, 1992) and that in this form they can successfully enhance self-esteem (Hajzler and Bernard, 1991).

Conclusions: rasing self-esteem – what works and what works best?

Despite the apparent immunity of established self-esteem to any evidence that challenges it, it is evident that low self-esteem can be raised by interventions intended to have this effect. Moreover, the evidence on the effectiveness of such interventions, although still limited, does allow us to go a little further than this. We can begin to answer some of the questions with which this chapter began.

How well do interventions work? The answer of course is: it depends. On average, effects of interventions are modest but they are distinctly stronger if the intervention was specifically intended to raise self-esteem and not to produce some other change believed, perhaps erroneously, to be a product of low self-esteem. This appears particularly the case for programmes aimed to reduce drug use among young people, for example. Interestingly, so far, some other factors have not been shown to influence the scale of effects, such as the length of the programme, the training and experience of those delivering it, or whether those for whom it is provided participate individually or in groups. Interventions also show clearer effects if participation versus non-participation is decided on a random basis. But there is an exception to this, the answer to the next question.

With which target groups do interventions work best? The clear answer here is that they work best for those identified with a relevant problem. They work less well as 'prevention' programmes. In other words, if the participants have relatively low self-esteem at the outset, their self-esteem is more likely to be raised than if their self-esteem is already at an average level.

Some of the other crucial questions remain to be answered. We know little about the long-term effects of interventions because they have been so seldom considered. Likewise, little is known about cost-effectiveness because evaluation studies have rarely involved direct comparisons of different kinds of intervention or treatment. Finally, we still know very little about why interventions work, though there are all kinds of promising hints that theories of self-esteem and research into its natural causes are sound bases for effective interventions. More progress might be made here through proper evaluation of process – without knowing what has been delivered and how, it is hard to make sense of what might be working and why. We need to know much more about each of these issues if interventions to raise self-esteem are to merit the investment of resources.

5 General conclusions

In the popular imagination, low self-esteem has become an all-purpose explanation for any significant social or personal problem, from crime to racism to drug abuse. Or, as Oprah Winfrey put it, nicely capturing the consensus position, lack of self-esteem is 'the root of all the problems in the world'. Its full range of supposedly baleful consequences have also been the subject of literally thousands of research studies. And, because the effects of low self-esteem have been assumed to be so damaging, there has been particular interest in identifying its causes and even greater enthusiasm for potential remedies.

One consequence of the enormous interest that social scientists have shown in this topic is that we are now able to move beyond popular supposition – in Smelser's terms, what we all know to be true – and take a reality check. And, though there are not yet clear answers to all the questions we may have, a more dispassionate appraisal reveals numerous faults with the popular view.

Defining and measuring self-esteem

The first requirements for good research are clear definitions of the variables at stake and sound procedures to measure these variables. Research into self-esteem has never been blessed with unanimity over definitions. Nonetheless, it has remained fairly close to the dictionary or common-sense definition – the opinion a person has of him or herself. The main point of difference is whether this opinion is primarily a general feeling (positive or negative) or a set of judgements as to whether and in what degree one has the various qualities one desires – good looks, moral virtue, social competence, artistic talents, intellectual skills. Or, as Coopersmith put it, self-esteem is the extent to which one judges oneself to be 'capable, significant, successful and worthy'.

These two interpretations have led to two kinds of measure. These two options, assessing respectively global feelings (Rosenberg's self-esteem measure, the RSE) and the separate components of self-evaluations (e.g. Coopersmith's measure), produce correlated assessments. But they are not identical and neither are the outcomes they predict. There have also been arguments about measurement methods; all the research examined in this review has relied upon self-reports. But these are cheap and simple to use and do work reasonably well and as yet there are no strong reasons to question their value.

Behavioural consequences of self-esteem

Self-esteem is potentially linked to behaviours in complex ways. The simplest possibility is that self-esteem has its own direct effect on behaviour. But the simplest possibility is only one of many. And these include the possibilities that self-esteem is either consequence rather than cause or that self-esteem and the behaviour of interest are both influenced by something else. Unfortunately, much research has not been up to the task of analysing these links adequately and is therefore virtually useless in answering the critical question: does self-esteem affect behaviour or not?

The most informative research for our purposes is prospective or longitudinal – it follows people over time and assesses the relevant variables at several time points. And it is multivariate – it assesses self-esteem but also several other variables that are plausibly influences on the outcomes of interest. Because this kind of research is expensive and requires a long-term commitment by researchers, there is relatively little of it. Another useful source of evidence therefore, if one which requires to be interpreted with caution, is experimental research. This includes the better-designed evaluations of interventions intended to raise self-esteem.

Bearing these qualifications in mind, the following conclusions are supported, albeit with varying degrees of certainty, by research (I concentrate here, as does most of the published research, on outcomes affecting young people – between the ages of ten and 25).

Young people with very low self-esteem are more likely to:

- show symptoms of depression; be more often unhappy

- become pregnant as teenagers (girls)

- have suicidal thoughts and make suicide attempts

- experience in their twenties longer periods of unemployment and earn less (males)

- suffer from eating disorders (if they are female)

- be victimised

- fail to respond to social influence

- have more difficulty forming and sustaining successful close relationships.

Young people with low self-esteem are not more likely as a result to:

- commit crimes, including violent crimes

- use or abuse illegal drugs

- drink alcohol to excess or smoke

- as parents, physically or sexually abuse their own children

- fail academically.

As a generalisation, it might be said that people who have or admit to low self-esteem – a poor opinion of themselves – treat themselves badly and may invite bad treatment by others. They do not, however, tend to treat others badly.

High self-esteem is therefore very unlikely to be the all-purpose social vaccine that some have supposed it to be. Indeed, it seems to have some disadvantages. Thus, young people with very high self-esteem are more likely to:

- hold prejudiced attitudes towards ethnic minorities

- reject social influence

- engage in physically risky pursuits.

There are other ways in which self-esteem may be implicated in behaviour but which have yet to be explored to any significant extent. Among these, perhaps the most interesting and potentially important is that self-esteem modifies the effect of other variables upon behaviour or outcomes such as physical health. Because self-esteem may even modify the direction of such effects, these influences will be more difficult to detect. One intriguing example suggests that positive life events enhance the health of those with high self-esteem but adversely affect the health of those with low self-esteem.

Finally, we need to recognise that self-esteem can be simultaneously cause and effect. Two examples here are victimisation and the quality of personal relationships.

The causes of low and high self-esteem

The most important influences on a person's level of self-esteem are their parents. This influence is partly genetic and partly produced by the degree of love, concern, acceptance and interest shown by parents through childhood and adolescence. Physical and particularly sexual abuse by parents has especially damaging and enduring effects. It also seems that after parents have had their say little else in life will be able to modify the opinion of self thus formed.

Indeed, one of the clearer messages of research concerns the relative immunity of established levels of self-esteem to disconfirming feedback. A range of strategies are deployed to discount any evidence that contradicts the opinions people have of themselves. These allow people to hold on to very positive opinions even when to the detached observer these would seem to have little basis. But the same strategies are also used by people with very low opinions of themselves to hold on to these estimations.

The operation of these strategies helps to clarify why so many conditions and circumstances do not have the impact on self-esteem that might otherwise be expected. The social prestige of the categories to which people belong have little or no effect on their self-esteem. This is true of social class and ethnicity. Being male confers a slight advantage over being female but the precise reasons for this have yet to be determined. Real successes and failures do have an effect but it is not large. Actual physical appearance – including both body shape and facial attractiveness – has far less impact on the individual than his or her self-image. Time and again it turns out that what matters is not the reality but what the individual believes to be the case. And this latter is often only tenuously related to the former.

The quality of close relationships with others does appear to be a significant determinant of self-esteem. But, as noted above, the likelihood of forming these relationships is itself a function of self-esteem.

Finally, self-esteem can be damaged by repeated, unambiguous and public failures and rejections – such as, for example, may be involved in being diagnosed an alcoholic, convicted for child abuse, or being unable to find employment. But it is not at all clear that there are correspondingly beneficial effects of public successes.

Planned interventions to raise self-esteem: what works?

Raising self-esteem is a massive and apparently profitable enterprise. It is also an enterprise without any strong inbuilt concern for proper evaluation. Consequently, our knowledge of what works and why is quite limited. But this is not to say we know nothing.

Some interventions undeniably do work – they produce measurable increases in self-esteem that cannot be attributed merely to the passage of time. What we can be less certain of is whether the gains achieved are sustained in the longer term; too few evaluations include long-term follow-ups.

It is also evident that some kinds of intervention work much better than others. But we do not know what it is about these interventions that makes them more or less successful. This is partly because there are few systematic replications. Any programme includes a host of elements that singly or in combination may be responsible for the programme's effects. Unless the programme is repeated, under varying conditions, the reasons for its effectiveness are likely to remain opaque.

More optimistically, however, programmes with a good grounding in theory and/or relevant research evidence consistently emerge as more effective. The message is that a well-founded understanding of the phenomenon one is trying to change will produce more effective efforts than facile intuitions of the 'positive feedback – good; negative feedback – bad' variety that permeate the self-esteem industry. Thus, research into the patterns of belief and the ways in which these are defended underpins the relative success of interventions based on cognitive-behavioural therapeutic techniques. Likewise, when the behavioural focus has been on outcomes affected, according to research evidence, by self-esteem, interventions have been more successful than when it has been on outcomes with no demonstrated link to self-esteem. Clear examples here are interventions to modify eating patterns compared to interventions to modify drug use.

But this brings us to the most conspicuous weakness to date of programme evaluations and to the very rationale for such programmes. We know next to nothing about the cost-effectiveness of interventions in this area. The efforts to raise self-esteem represented by so many programmes, projects and therapies are not driven primarily by the belief that high self-esteem is desirable in its own right. Rather, it is to be desired because of the benefits it delivers.

We have seen that many of these supposed benefits are illusory and this weakens the case for investing in high self-esteem as a general-purpose social vaccine. There may, however, be some specific benefits. The following question must therefore arise: is it more efficient to concentrate on raising self-esteem or on achieving these benefits more directly? An obvious example here is risk of teenage pregnancy. Low self-esteem appears to be a risk factor but improving the knowledge and skills required to use contraception effectively may nonetheless be a more cost-effective way of reducing the risk.

Future research needs

One hesitates to argue for more research when studies are already being published at a rate that threatens to overwhelm our capacity to register their conclusions, let alone absorb their implications. There is nevertheless a strong case for more *good* research. As noted above with respect to consequences of self-esteem, this includes longitudinal and multivariate research adequate to the task of teasing out the potentially quite complex ways in which self-esteem might be implicated in these consequences.

Research designs, and the analyses of the data generated by these designs, need to be capable of detecting moderator effects and non-linear relationships. The evidence regarding conformity and persuasion is an important lesson here. In this case, the clear difference turns out to be between those whose self-esteem is moderate and those whose self-esteem is either very high or very low.

Turning to more specific research questions, there are five links with self-esteem that merit further clarification, those with teenage pregnancy, eating disorders, victimisation, quality of personal

relationships and adult economic circumstances. The case of victimisation is interesting because the link appears to be reciprocal, as it does for quality of personal relationships. With respect to teenage pregnancy, low self-esteem does seem to be a significant risk factor but it is one among several. It is not clear how it generates the risk or how it interacts with other factors. Similar uncertainties remain with respect to eating disorders. Finally, the apparent consequences of low self-esteem in childhood for economic circumstances in the twenties is intriguing and not at all straightforward. But the scale of the effects found are such as to merit further inquiry.

Whether any of these questions are in the end adequately addressed will depend on the conviction that the answers are worth having. Expensive research is not necessarily good research but good research is not likely to be cheap. But evidence-based practice is surely as desirable in the domain of mental health and well-being as it is in medicine. And, just as surely, good research to provide this evidence would be a better investment of our resources than unproven treatments promising illusory benefits.

Final word

It is worth remembering that our language contains many other words to describe people with high self-esteem – narcissistic, big-headed, braggarts, boastful, arrogant, smug, self-satisfied, vain, conceited – and that these reflect the wisdom of culturally accumulated experience: there is also a downside to very high self-esteem. It is not an unconditional benefit. Recall the evidence on racism, violence and risk taking. Perhaps we should be more willing to acknowledge that very high self-esteem, as much as self-esteem that is exceptionally low, is a problem in need of treatment, and more open-minded to the benefits of moderation.

Chapter 1

1 There are versions that expand upon the alternative responses allowed so that degrees of agreement can be signalled. This effectively also extends the scale, from 10 to 50 or more points.

Chapter 2

1 In this and succeeding sections considering the possible consequences of low self-esteem, a more extensive discussion of the research evidence upon which the conclusions are based is provided in the Appendix.

Chapter 3

1 The researchers also checked that these events were perceived as positive. However, these kinds of major life events also entail changes for the person to whom they happen and any kind of change carries with it an element of stress. It may be, therefore, that the associated stress, however positive the events may feel, has effects that interact with self-esteem.

Bibliography

Aberson, C., Healy, M. and Romero, V. (2000) 'Ingroup bias and self-esteem: a meta-analytic review', *Personality and Social Psychology Review*, Vol. 4, pp. 157–73

Abood, D.A. and Conway, T.L. (1988) *Health Value and Self-esteem as Predictors of Wellness Behaviors*. US Naval Health Research Center Report No. 89-27

Abrams, K.K., Allen, L.R. and Gray, J.J. (1993) 'Disordered eating attitudes and behaviors, psychological adjustment and ethnic identity: a comparison of black and white female college students', *International Journal of Eating Disorders*, Vol. 14, pp. 49–57

Ager, J.W., Sheam F.P. and Agronow, S.J. (1982) 'Method discontinuance in teenage women: implications for teen contraception programs', in I.R. Stuart and C.F. Wells (eds) *Pregnancy in Adolescence: Needs, Problems and Management*. New York: Van Nostrand Reinhold

Ahlgren, A., Norem, A.A., Hochhauser, M. and Garvin, J. (1982) 'Antecedents of smoking among pre-adolescents', *Journal of Drug Education*, Vol. 12, pp. 325–40

Altemeyer, B. (1996) *The Authoritarian Specter*. Cambrige, MA: Harvard University Press

Anderson, S.C. and Lauderdale, M.L. (1982) 'Characteristics of abusive parents: a look at self-esteem', *Child Abuse and Neglect*, Vol. 6, pp. 285–93

Andrews, B. and Brown, G. (1995) 'Stability and change in low self-esteem: the role of psychosocial factors', *Psychological Medicine*, Vol. 25, pp. 23–31

Andrews, J.A. and Duncan, S.C. (1997) 'Examining the reciprocal relation between academic motivation and substance use: effects of family relationships, self-esteem and general deviance', *Journal of Behavioral Medicine*, Vol. 20, pp. 523–49

Armistead, L., Forehand, R., Beach, S.R.H. and Brody, G.H. (1995) 'Predicting interpersonal competence in young adulthood: the roles of family, self and peer systems during adolescence', *Journal of Child and Family Studies*, Vol. 4, pp. 445–60

Aron, A., Paris, M. and Aron, E.N. (1995) 'Falling in love: prospective studies of self-concept change', *Journal of Personality and Social Psychology*, Vol. 69, pp. 1102–12

Azmitia, M., Lippman, D.N. and Ittel, A. (1999) 'On the relation of personal experience to early adolescents' reasoning about best friend deterioration', *Social Development*, Vol. 8, pp. 275–91

Baldwin, M.W. and Keelan, J.P.R. (1999) 'Interpersonal expectations as a function of self-esteem and sex', *Journal of Social and Personal Relationships*, Vol. 16, pp. 822–33

Barkham, M., Rees, A., Shapiro, D.A., Stiles, W.B. *et al.* (1996) 'Outcomes of time-limited psychotherapy in applied settings: replicating the second Sheffield psychotherapy project', *Journal of Consulting and Clinical Psychology*, Vol. 64, pp. 1079–85

Baron, R.M. and Kenny, D.A. (1986) 'The mediator–moderator variable distinction in social psychological research: conceptual, strategic and statistical considerations', *Journal of Personality and Social Psychology*, Vol. 51, pp. 1173–82

Barth, R.P., Schinke, S.P. and Maxwell, J.S. (1983) 'Psychological correlates of teenage motherhood', *Journal of Youth and Adolescence*, Vol. 12, pp. 471–87

Baumeister, R. (1998) 'The self', in D. Gilbert, S. Fiske and G. Lindzey (eds) *Handbook of Social Psychology*, Vol. 1, 4th edition. New York: McGraw-Hill, pp. 694–700

Baumeister, R., Smart, L. and Boden, J. (1996) 'Relation of threatened egoism to violence and aggression: the dark side of high self esteem', *Psychological Review*, Vol. 103, pp. 5–33

Baumeister, R., Tice, D. and Hutton, D. (1989) 'Self presentational motives and personality differences in self esteem', *Journal of Personality*, Vol. 57, pp. 547–79

Beamer, L.J. (1999) 'Psychological and sociocultural determinants of a preoccupation with thinness in college women', unpublished doctoral dissertation, State University of New York at Albany

Beautrais, A.L., Joyce, P.R. and Mulder, R.T. (1999) 'Personality traits and cognitive styles as risk factors for serious suicide attempts among young people', *Suicide and Life Threatening Behavior*, Vol. 29, pp. 37–47

Becker, H. (1963) *Outsiders*. New York: Free Press

Beckman, L.J. (1978) 'Self-esteem of women alcoholics', *Journal of Studies on Alcohol*, Vol. 39, pp. 491–8

Bednar, R.L., Wells, M.G. and Peterson, S.R. (1989) *Self esteem: Paradoxes and Innovations in Clinical Theory and Practice*. Washington, DC: American Psychological Association

Beer, J. and Beer, J. (1992) 'Depression, self-esteem, suicide ideation and GPAs of high school students at risk', *Psychological Reports*, Vol. 71, pp. 899–902

Biggs, S.J., Bender, M.P. and Forean, J. (1983) 'Are there psychological differences between persistent solvent-abusing delinquents and delinquents who do not abuse solvents?', *Journal of Adolescence*, Vol. 6, pp. 71–86

Bishop, J.A. and Inderbitzen, H.M. (1995) 'Peer acceptance and friendship: an investigation of their relation to self-esteem', *Journal of Early Adolescence*, Vol. 15, pp. 476–89

Blaskovich, J. and Tomaka, J. (1991) 'Measures of self esteem', in J.P. Robinson, P.R. Shaver and L.S. Wrightsman (eds) *Measures of Personality and Social Psychological Attitudes*. San Diego, CA: Academic Press, pp. 115–60

Bohrnstedt, G.W. and Felson, R.B. (1983) 'Explaining the relations among children's actual and perceived performances and self-esteem: a comparison of several causal models', *Journal of Personality and Social Psychology*, Vol. 45, pp. 43–56

Botvin, G.J., Baker, E., Goldberg, C.J., Dusenbury, L. *et al.* (1992) 'Correlates and predictors of smoking among black adolescents', *Addictive Behaviors*, Vol. 17, pp. 97–103

Boudewyn, A.C. and Liem, J.H. (1995) 'Psychological, interpersonal and behavioral correlates of chronic self-destructiveness: an exploratory study', *Psychological Reports*, Vol. 77, pp. 1283–97

Brockner, J. (1988) *Self-esteem at Work: Research, Theory and Practice*. Lexington, MA: Lexington Books

Brown, G., Bifulco, A.T., Veiel, H.O. and Andrews, B. (1990) 'Self-esteem and depression: II. Social correlates of self-esteem', *Social Psychiatry and Psychiatric Epidemiology*, Vol. 26, pp. 225–34

Brown, J. (1993) 'Self-esteem and self-evaluations: feeling is believing', in J. Suls (ed.) *Psychological Perspectives on the Self*, Vol. 4. Hillsdale, NJ: Erlbaum

Brown, J.D. and McGill, K.L. (1989) 'The costs of good fortune: when positive life events produce negative health consequences', *Journal of Personality and Social Psychology*, Vol. 57, pp. 1103–10

Brown, R. (2000) 'Social identity theory: past achievements, current problems and future challenges', *European Journal of Social Psychology*, Vol. 30, pp. 745–78

Browne, A. and Finkelor, D. (1986) 'Impact of child sexual abuse: a review of the research', *Psychological Bulletin*, Vol. 99, pp. 66–77

Brunswick, A. (1971) 'Adolescent health, sex and fertility', *Adolescent Sexuality*, Vol. 61, pp. 711–29

Bry, B.H. (1983) 'Substance abuse in women: etiology and prevention', *Issues in Mental Health Nursing*, Vol. 5, pp. 253–72

Buhrmester, D., Furman, W., Wittenberg, M.T. and Reis, H.T. (1988) 'Five domains of interpersonal competence in peer relations', *Journal of Personality and Social Psychology*, Vol. 55, pp. 991–1008

Button, E.J., Sonuga-Barke, E.J., Davies, J. and Thompson, M. (1996) 'A prosepctive study of self-esteem in the prediction of eating problems in adolescent schoolgirls: questionnaire findings', *British Journal of Clinical Psychology*, Vol. 35, pp. 193–203

Bynner, J., O'Malley, P.M. and Bachman, J.G. (1981) 'Self-esteem and delinquency revisited', *Journal of Youth and Adolescence*, Vol. 10, pp. 407–44

Calam, R. and Waller, G. (1998) 'Are eating and psychosocial characteristics in early teenage years useful predictors of eating characteristics in early adulthood? A 7-year longitudinal study', *International Journal of Eating Disorders*, Vol. 24, pp. 351–62

California Task Force to Promote Self-esteem and Personal and Social Responsibility (1990) *Toward a State of Self-esteem*. Sacramento, CA: California State Department of Education

Canals, J., Carbajo, G., Fernandez, J., Marti-Henneberg, C. and Domenech, E. (1996) 'Biopsychopathological risk profiles of adolescents with eating disorder symptoms', *Adolescence*, Vol. 31, pp. 443–50

Caputo, R.K. (1998) 'Economic well-being in a youth cohort', *Families in Society*, Vol. 79, pp. 83–92

Carroll, J.F.X., Malloy, T.E., Roscioli, D.L., Pindjalk G.M. and Clifford, J.S. (1982) 'Similarities and differences in self-concepts of women alcoholics and drug addicts', *Journal of Studies on Alcohol*, Vol. 43, pp. 725–38

Carvajal, S.C., Clair, S.D., Nash, S.G. and Evans, R.I. (1998) 'Relating optimism, hope and self esteem to social influences in deterring substance use in adolescents', *Journal of Social and Clinical Psychology*, Vol. 17, pp. 433–65

Charalampous, K.D., Ford, K.B and Skinner, T.J. (1976) 'Self esteem in alcoholics and non-alcoholics', *Journal of Studies on Alcohol*, Vol. 37, pp. 990–4

Christensen, M.J., Brayden, R.M., Dietrich, M.S., McLaughlin, F.J., Sharrod, K.A. and Altemeier, W.A. (1994) 'The prospective assessment of self-concept on neglectful and physically abusive low-income mothers', *Child Abuse and Neglect*, Vol. 18, pp. 222–32

Conrad, K.M., Flay, B.R. and Hill, D. (1992) 'Why children start smoking cigarettes: predictors of onset', *British Journal of Addiction*, Vol. 87, pp. 1711–24

Cookson, H. (1994) 'Personality variables associated with alcohol use in young offenders', *Personality and Individual Differences*, Vol. 16, pp. 179–82

Cooley, C.H. (1902) *Human Nature and the Social Order*. New York: Scribner

Coombs, R.H., Santana, F.O. and Fawzy, F.I. (1984) 'Parent training to prevent adolescent drug use: an educational model', *Journal of Drug Issues*, Vol. 14, pp. 393–402

Coopersmith, S. (1967) *The Antecedents of Self-esteem*. San Francisco, CA: W.H. Freeman

Coric, D. and Murstein, B.I. (1993) 'Bulimia nervosa: prevalence and psychological correlates in a college community', *Eating Disorders: The Journal of Treatment and Prevention*, Vol. 1, pp. 39–51

Covington, M.V. (1989) 'Self esteem and failure in school: analysis and policy implications', in A.M. Mecca, N. Smelser and J. Vasconcellos (eds) *The Social Importance of Self Esteem*. Berkeley, CA: University of California Press

Cramer, D. (1990) 'Disclosure of personal problems, self-esteem and the facilitativeness of friends and lovers', *British Journal of Guidance and Counselling*, Vol. 18, pp. 186–96

Crockenberg, S.B. and Soby, B.A. (1989) 'Self-esteem and teenage pregnancy', in A.M. Mecca, N. Smelser and J. Vasconcellos (eds) *The Social Importance of Self Esteem*. Berkeley, CA: University of California Press

Crocker, J. and Major, B. (1989) 'Social stigma and self esteem: the self-protective properties of stigma', *Psychological Review*, Vol. 96, pp. 608–30

Crocker, J. and Schwartz, L. (1985) 'Prejudice and ingroup favoritism in a minimal intergroup situation: effects of self-esteem', *Personality and Social Psychology Bulletin*, Vol. 11, pp. 379–86

Culp, R.E., Culp, A.M., Soulis, J. and Letts, D. (1989) 'Self-esteem and depression in abusive, neglecting and nonmaltreating mothers', *Infant Mental Health Journal*, Vol. 10, pp. 243–51

Cvetkovich, G. and Grote, B. (1980) 'Psychosocial development and the social problem of teenage illegitimacy', in C. Chilman (ed.) *Adolescent Pregnancy and Childbearing: Findings from Research*. Washington, DC: US Department of Health and Human Services

Darnall, B.D., Smith, J.E., Craighead, L.W. and Lamaunier, J.A. (1999) 'Modification of the cognitive model for bulimia via path analysis in a Brazilian adolescent sample', *Addictive Behaviours*, Vol. 21, pp. 47–57

De Man, A.F. (1999) 'Correlates of suicide ideation in high school students: the importance of depression', *Journal of Genetic Psychology*, Vol. 160, pp. 105–14

De Man, A.F., Leduc, C.P. and Labreche-Gauthier, L. (1992) 'Correlates of suicide ideation in French-Canadian adults and adolescents: a comparison', *Journal of Clinical Psychology*, Vol. 48, pp. 811–16

De Man, A.F., Leduc, C.P. and Labreche-Gauthier, L. (1993) 'Correlates of suicide ideation in French-Canadian adolescents: personal variables, stress and social support', *Adolescence*, Vol. 28, pp. 819–30

Dembo, R., Dertke, M., La-Voie, L., Borders, S. *et al.* (1987) 'Physical abuse, sexual victimization and illicit drug use: a structural analysis among high risk adolescents', *Journal of Adolescence*, Vol. 10, pp. 13–34

Demo, D.H. (1985) 'The measurement of self-esteem: refining our methods', *Journal of Personality and Social Psychology*, Vol. 48, pp. 1490–502

Dennison, S. (2000) 'A win–win peer mentoring and tutoring program: a collaborative model', *Journal of Primary Prevention*, Vol. 20, pp. 161–74

De Ronde, C. and Swann, W.B.(1993) 'Caught in the cross-fire: positivity and self-verification strivings among people with low self-esteem', in R.F. Baumeister (ed.) *Self-esteem: The Puzzle of Low Self-regard*. New York: Plenum

Diekstra, R.F., Kienhorst, C.W. and de Wilde, E.J. (1995) 'Suicide and suicidal behaviour among adolescents', in M. Rutter and D.J. Smith (eds) *Psychosocial Disorders in Young People*. Chichester: Wiley

Dielman, T.E., Leech, S.L., Lorenger, A.T. and Horvath, W.J. (1984) 'Health locus of control and self-esteem as related to adolescent health behavior and intentions', *Adolescence*, Vol. 19, pp. 935–50

Dielman, T.E., Shope, J.T., Leech, S.L. and Butchart, A.T. (1989) 'Differential effectiveness of an elementary school-based alcohol misuse prevention program by type of prior drinking experience', *Journal of School Health*, Vol. 59, pp. 255–63

Dishion, T.J., Patterson, G.R. and Reid, J.R. (1988) *Parent and Peer Factors Associated with Drug Sampling in Early Adolescence: Implications for Treatment*. National Institute on Drug Abuse, Research Monograph Series, No. 77, pp. 69–93

Dolgin, K.G., Meyer, L. and Schwartz, J. (1991) 'Effects of gender, target's gender, topic and self-esteem on disclosure to best and middling friends', *Sex Roles*, Vol. 25, pp. 311–29

Dollard, J., Dob, L., Miller, N., Mowrer, O. and Sears, R. (1939) *Frustration and Aggression*. New Haven, CT: Yale University Press

Dooley, D. and Prause, J. (1995) 'Effect of unemployment on school leavers' self-esteem', *Journal of Occupational and Organizational Psychology*, Vol. 68, pp. 177–92

Dooley, D. and Prause, J. (1997) 'Effect of students' self-esteem on later employment status: interactions of self-esteem with gender and race', *Applied Psychology: An International Review*, Vol. 46, pp. 175–98

Drummond, R.J. and Hansford, S.G. (1991) 'Dimensions of self-concept of pregnant unwed teens', *Journal of Psychology*, Vol. 125, pp. 65–9

Durham, R.C., Murphy, T., Allan, T., Richard, K. *et al.* (1994) 'Cognitive therapy, analytic psychotherapy and anxiety management training for generalised anxiety disorder', *British Journal of Psychiatry*, Vol. 165, pp. 315–23

Eagly, A. and Chaiken, S. (1993) *The Psychology of Attitudes*. Fort Worth, TX: Harcourt Brace

Egan, S.K. and Perry, D.D. (1998) 'Does low self-regard invite victimization?', *Developmental Psychology*, Vol. 34, pp. 299–309

Ellis, A. (1973) 'Rational-emotive therapy', in R.J. Corsini (ed.) *Current Psychotherapies*. Itasca, IL: Peacock Publishers

Emler, N. (2000) 'Social structures and individual lives: effects of participation in the institutions of family, education and work', in J. Bynner and R. Silbereisen (eds) *Adversity and Challenge in England and in the New Germany*. London: Macmillan

Emler, N. and Frazer, E. (1999) 'Politics: the education effect', *Oxford Review of Education*, Vol. 25, pp. 251–74

Emler, N. and Reicher, S. (1995) *Adolescence and Delinquency: The Collective Management of Reputation*. Oxford: Blackwell

Emler, N., Cook, T. and St James, A. (2000) 'Interpersonal perceptions in acquainted groups', unpublished manuscript, Oxford University

Ennett, S.T., Rosenbaum, D.T., Flewelling, R.L., Bieler, G.S. *et al.* (1994) 'Long-term evaluation of drug abuse resistance education', *Addictive Behaviors*, Vol. 19, pp. 113–25

Epstein, S. (1979) 'The ecological study of emotions in humans', in K. Blankstein (ed.) *Advances in the Study of Communication and Affect*. New York: Plenum

Evans, A.L., (1980) 'Personality characteristics and disciplinary attitudes of child-abusing mothers', *Child Abuse and Neglect*, Vol. 4, pp. 179–87

Farnham, S.D., Greenwald, A.G. and Banaji, M.R. (1999) 'Implicit self-esteem', in D. Abrams and M. Hogg (eds) *Social Identity and Social Cognition*. Oxford: Blackwell

Feinstein, L. (2000) 'The relative economic importance of academic, psychological and behavioural attributes developed in childhood', unpublished paper, Centre for Economic Performance, London School of Economics

Feiring, C. and Taska, L.S. (1996) 'Family self-concept: ideas on its meaning', in B. Braken (ed.) *Handbook of Self-concept*. New York: Wiley

Ferroni, P. and Taffe, J. (1997) 'Women's emotional well-being: the importance of communicating sexual needs', *Sexual and Marital Therapy*, Vol. 12, pp. 127–38

Feshbach, S. (1971) 'The dynamics and morality of violence and aggression', *American Psychologist*, Vol. 26, pp. 281–92

Festinger, L. (1954) 'A theory of social comparison processes', *Human Relations*, Vol. 7, pp. 117–40

Fidler, W., Michell, L., Raab, G. and Charlton, A. (1992) 'Smoking: a special need?', *British Journal of Addiction*, Vol. 87, pp. 1583–91

Field, T., Lang, C., Yando, R. and Bendell, D. (1995) 'Adolescents' intimacy with parents and friends', *Adolescence*, Vol. 30, pp. 133–40

Finke, L. and Williams, J. (1999) 'Alcohol and drug use of inner-city versus rural school age children', *Journal of Drug Education*, Vol. 29, pp. 279–91

Fisher, D., Beech, A. and Browne, K. (1999) 'Comparison of sex offenders to nonoffenders on selected psychological measures', *International Journal of Offender Therapy and Comparative Criminology*, Vol. 43, pp. 473–91

Fisher, M., Pastore, D., Schneider, M., Pegler, C. *et al.* (1994) 'Eating attitudes in urban and suburban adolescents', *International Journal of Eating Disorders*, Vol. 16, pp. 67–74

Fitts, W.H. (1965) *Tennessee Self Concept Scale*. Nashville, TN: Counselor Recordings and Tests, Department of Mental Health

Fleming, J.S. and Courtney, B.E. (1984) 'The dimensionality of self esteem, II: Hierarchical facet model for revised measurement scales', *Journal of Personality and Social Psychology*, Vol. 46, pp. 442–52

Fombonne, E. (1995) 'Eating disorders: time trends and possible explanatory mechanisms', in M. Rutter and D.J. Smith (eds) *Psychosocial Disorders in Young People*. Chichester: Wiley

Fordham, K. and Hinde, J.S. (1999) 'Shyness, friendship quality and adjustment during middle childhood', *Journal of Child Psychology, Psychiatry and Allied Disciplines*, Vol. 40, pp. 757–68

Franco, N. and Levitt, M.J. (1998) 'The social ecology of middle childhood: family support, friendship quality and self-esteem', *Family Relations: Interdisciplinary Journal of Applied Family Studies*, Vol. 47, pp. 315–21

Franklin, J.T. (1985) 'Alternative education as substance abuse prevention', *Journal of Alcohol and Drug Education*, Vol. 30, pp. 12–23

Frederick, C.M. and Grow, V.M. (1996) 'A mediational model of autonomy, self-esteem and eating disordered attitudes and behaviors', *Psychology of Women Quarterly*, Vol. 20, pp. 217–28

Friedman, H.L. (1989) 'The health of adolescents: beliefs and behaviour', *Social Science and Medicine*, Vol. 29, pp. 309–15

Furnham, A. and Calman, A. (1998) 'Eating disturbance, self esteem, reasons for exercising and body weight dissatisfaction in adolescent males', *European Eating Disorders Review*, Vol. 6, pp. 58–72

Furnham, A. and Lowick, V. (1984) 'Lay theories of the causes of alcoholism', *British Journal of Medical Psychology*, Vol. 57, pp. 319–32

Fryer, S., Waller, G. and Kroese, B.S. (1997) 'Stress, coping and disturbed eating attitudes in teenage girls', *International Journal of Eating Disorders*, Vol. 22, pp. 427–36

Garnefski, N., Diekstra, R.F. and Heus, P. (1992) 'A population-based survey of the characteristics of high school students with and without a history of suicidal behavior', *Acta Psychiatrica Scandinavica*, Vol. 86, pp. 189–96

Garner, D.M., Rokert, W., Davis, R., Garner, M.V. *et al.* (1993) 'Comparison of cognitive-behavioural and supportive expressive therapy for bulimia nervosa', *American Journal of Psychiatry*, Vol. 150, pp. 37–46

Garris, L., Stecker, A. and McIntire, J.R. (1976) 'The relationship between oral contraceptives and adolescent sexual behavior', *Journal of Sex Research*, Vol. 12, pp. 135–46

Ghaderi, A. and Scott, B. (1999) 'Prevalence and psychological correlates of eating disorders among femles aged 18–30 years in the general population', *Acta Psychiatrica Scandinavica*, Vol. 99, pp. 261–6

Ghadirian, A.M. (1979) 'Adolescent acloholism: motives and alternatives', *Comprehensive Psychiatry*, Vol. 20, pp. 469–74

Ghindia, D.J. and Kola, L.A. (1996) 'Co-factors affecting substance abuse among homosexual men: an investigation within a midwestern gay community', *Drug and Alcohol Dependence*, Vol. 41, pp. 167–77

Gillies, V., McCarthy, J.P. and Holland, J. (2001) *Pulling Together, Pulling Apart: The Family Lives of Young People.* York: Joseph Rowntree Foundation

Giordano, P.C., Cernkovich, S.A., Groat, H.T., Pugh, M.D. and Swinford, S.P. (1998) 'The quality of adolescent friendships: long term effects?', *Journal of Health and Social Behavior*, Vol. 39, pp. 55–71

Glanz, M.D. and Pickens, R.W. (1992) 'Vulnerability to drug abuse: introduction and overview', in M.D. Glanz and R.W. Pickens (eds) *Vulnerability to Drug Abuse.* Washington, DC: American Psychological Association

Goddard, E. (1990) *Why Children Start Smoking.* London: HMSO/OPCS

Gold, M. and Mann, D. (1972) 'Delinquency as defense', *American Journal of Orthopsychiatry*, Vol. 42, pp. 463–79

Goldney, R.D., Smith, S., Winefield, A.H., Tiggerman, M. *et al.* (1991) 'Suicidal ideation: its enduring nature and associated morbidity', *Acta Psychiatrica Scandinavica*, Vol. 83, pp. 115–20

Goldsmith, A.H., Veum, J.R. and Darity, W. (1996) 'The impact of labor force history on self-esteem and its component parts, anxiety, alienation and depression', *Journal of Economic Psychology*, Vol. 17, pp. 183–220

Goldsmith, A.H., Veum, J.R. and Darity, W. (1997) 'Unemployment, joblessness, psychological well-being and self-esteem: theory and evidence', *Journal of Socio-Economics*, Vol. 26, pp. 133–58

Gonzalez, F.C., Garcia, G. and Medina-Mora, M.E. (1998) 'Indicadores psicosociales predictores de ideacion suicida en dos generaciones de estudiantes universitarios', *Salud Mental*, Vol. 21, pp. 1–9

Gordon, W.R. and Caltabiano, M.L. (1996) 'Urban–rural differences in adolescent self-esteem, leisure boredom and sensation seeking as predictors of leisure time usage and satisfaction', *Adolescence*, Vol. 31, pp. 883–901

Gray-Little, B. and Hafdahl, A. (2000) 'Factors influencing racial comparisons of self esteem: a quantitative review', *Psychological Bulletin*, Vol. 126, pp. 26–54

Green, A.H., Gains, R.W. and Sandgrund, A. (1974) 'Child abuse: pathological syndrome of family interaction', *American Journal of Psychiatry*, Vol. 131, pp. 882–6

Greenwald, A. and Banaji, M. (1995) 'Implicit social cognition: attitudes, self-esteem and stereotypes', *Psychological Review*, Vol. 102, pp. 4–27

Griffiths, R.A., Beumont, P.J.V., Giannakopoulos, E., Russell, J., Schotte, D., Thornton, C., Touyz, S.W. and Varano, P. (1999) 'Measuring self esteem in dieting disordered patients: the validity of the Rosenberg and Coopersmith contrasted', *International Journal of Eating Disorders*, Vol. 25, pp. 227–31

Gross, W.F. and Adler, L.O. (1970) 'Aspects of alcoholics' self-concepts as measured by the Tennessee self-concept scale', *Psychological Reports*, Vol. 27, pp. 431–4

Grubb, H.J., Sellers, M.I. and Waligroski, K. (1993) 'Factors related to depression and eating disorders: self-esteem, body image and attractiveness', *Psychological Reports*, Vol. 72, pp. 1003–10

Gutierres, S.E. and Reich, J.W. (1988) 'Attributional analysis of drug abuse and gender: effects of treatment and relationship to rehabilitation', *Journal of Social and Clinical Psychology*, Vol. 7, pp. 176–91

Hajzler, D.J. and Bernard, M.E. (1991) 'A review of rational-emotive education outcome studies', *School Psychology Quarterly*, Vol. 6, pp. 27–49

Hamilton, A., Stiles, W.B., Melowsky, F. and Beal, D.G. (1987) 'A multilevel comparison of child abusers with nonabusers', *Journal of Family Violence*, Vol. 2, pp. 215–25

Haney, P. and Durlak, J.A. (1998) 'Changing self-esteem in children and adolescents: a meta-analytic review', *Journal of Clinical Child Psychology*, Vol. 27, pp. 423–33

Hansford, B.C. and Hattie, J.A. (1982) 'The relationship between self and achievement/ performance motivation', *Review of Educational Research*, Vol. 52, pp. 123–42

Harmon, M.A. (1993) 'Reducing the risk of drug involvement among early adolescents: an evaluation of Drug Abuse Resistance Education (DARE), *Evaluation Review*, Vol. 17, pp. 221–39

Harrison, B.G. (1989) 'The importance of being Oprah', *The New York Times Magazine*, 11 June, pp. 28–30

Hart, D., Fegley, S. and Brengelman, D. (1993) 'Perceptions of past, present and future selves among children and adolescents', *British Journal of Developmental Psychology*, Vol. 11, pp. 265–82

Hart, D., Hoffman, V., Edelstein, W. and Keller, M. (1997) 'The relationship of childhood personality types to adolescent behavior and development: a longitudinal study of Icelandic children', *Developmental Psychology*, Vol. 33, pp. 195–205

Harter, S. (1993) 'Causes and consequences of low self-esteem in children and adolescents', in R.F. Baumeister (ed.) *Self-esteem: The Puzzle of Low Self-regard*. New York: Plenum

Harter, S. (1998) 'The development of self-representations', in W. Damon and N. Eisenberg (eds) *Handbook of Child Psychology, Vol. 3, Social, Emotional and Personality Development*, 5th ed. New York: Wiley

Hawker, D.S. and Boulton, M.J. (2000) 'Twenty years' research on peer victimization and psychosocial maladjustment: a meta-analytic review of cross-sectional studies', *Journal of Child Psychology and Psychiatry and Allied Disciplines*, Vol. 41, pp. 441–55

Hays, R.D., Stacy, A.W., Widaman, K.F., Dimatteo, M.R. *et al.* (1986) 'Multistage path models of adolescent alcohol and drug use: a reanalysis', *Journal of Drug Issues*, Vol. 16, pp. 357–69

Hendin, H. (1974) 'Beyond alienation: the end of the psychedelic road', *American Journal of Drug and Alcohol Abuse*, Vol. 1, pp. 11–23

Hernandez, J. (1995) 'The concurrence of eating disorders with histories of child abuse among adolescents', *Journal of Child Sexual Abuse*, Vol. 4, pp. 73–85

Herrenkohl, E.C., Herrenkohl, R.C., Egolf, B.P. and Russo, M J. (1998) 'The relationship between early maltreatment and teenage parenthood', *Journal of Adolescence*, Vol. 21, pp. 291–303

Herrold, E.S. and Goodwin, M.S. (1979) 'Self-esteem and sexual permissiveness', *Journal of Clinical Psychology*, Vol. 35, pp. 908-12

Herrold, E.S., Goodwin, M.S. and Lero, D.S. (1979) 'Self-esteem, locus of control and adolescent contraception', *Journal of Psychology*, Vol. 101, pp. 83–8

Hershberger, S.L., Pilkington, N.W. and D'Augelli, A.R. (1997) 'Predictors of suicide attempts among gay, lesbian and bisexual youth', *Journal of Adolescent Research*, Vol. 12, pp. 447–97

Hesse-Biber, S., Marino, M. and Watts-Roy, D. (1999) 'A longitudinal study of eating disorders among college women: factors that influence recovery', *Gender and Society*, Vol. 13, pp. 385–408

Hetherton, T.F. and Polivy, J. (1991) 'Development and validation of a scale for measuring state self-esteem', *Journal of Personality and Social Psychology*, Vol. 60, pp. 895–910

Hewitt, J.P. (1998) *The Myth of Self-esteem: Finding Happiness and Solving Problems in America*. New York: St Martin's Press

Hoge, D., Smit, E. and Crist, J. (1995) 'Reciprocal effects of self-concept and academic achievement in sixth and seventh grade', *Journal of Youth and Adolescence*, Vol. 24, pp. 295–314

Hollar, D.S. and Snizek, W.E. (1996) 'The influences of knowledge of HIV/AIDS and self-esteem on the sexual practices of college students', *Social Behavior and Personality*, Vol. 24, pp. 75–86

Hollon, S.D. and Garber, J. (1990) 'Cognitive therapy for depression: a social cognitive perspective', *Personality and Social Psychology Bulletin*, Vol. 16, pp. 58–73

Hopkins, R.H., Mauss, A.L., Kearney, K.A. and Weisheit, R.A. (1988) 'Comprehensive evaluation of a model alcohol education curriculum', *Journal of Studies on Alcohol*, Vol. 49, pp. 38–50

Hornick, J.P., Doran, L. and Crawford, S.H. (1979) 'Premarital contraceptive usage among male and female adolescents', *Family Coordinator*, Vol. 11, pp. 181–90

Horowitz, L.A. (1999) 'The relationship of childhood sexual abuse to revictimization: mediating variables and developmental processes', unpublished doctoral dissertation, Catholic University of America

Howard, M.O. and Jenson, J.M. (1999) 'Inhalant use among anitsocial youth: prevalence and correlates', *Addictive Behaviors*, Vol. 24, pp. 59–74

Hubbard, S.T., Gray, J.J. and Parker, S. (1998) 'Differences among women who exercise for "food related" and "non-food related" reasons', *European Eating Disorders Review*, Vol. 6, pp. 225–65

Hurry, J. and McGurk, H. (1997) 'An evaluation of a primary prevention programme for schools', *Addiction Research*, Vol. 5, pp. 23–38

Iannos, M. and Tiggeman, M. (1997) 'Personality and the excessive exerciser', *Personality and Individual Differences*, Vol. 22, pp. 775–8

Jackson, C., Henriksoen, L., Dickinson, D., Messer, L. and Robertson, S.B. (1998) 'A longitudinal study predicting patterns of cigarette smoking among children and adolescents', *Health Education and Behavior*, Vol. 25, pp. 319–37

James, W. (1890) *Principles of Psychology*. New York: Dover

Jang, S.J. and Thornberry, T.P. (1998) 'Self-esteem, delinquent peers and delinqeucy: a test of the self-enhancement thesis', *American Sociological Review*, Vol. 63, pp. 568–98

Janis, I. and Field, P.B. (1959) 'A behavioral assessment of persuasability: consistency of individual differences', in C.I. Hovland and I.L. Janis (eds) *Personality and Persuasability*. New Haven, CT: Yale University Press, pp. 55–68

Jensen, G.F. (1973) 'Inner containment and delinquency', *Journal of Criminal Law and Criminology*, Vol. 64, pp. 464–70

Jessor, S.L. and Jessor, R. (1975) 'Transition from virginity to nonvirginity among youth: a social-psychological study over time', *Developmental Psychology*, Vol. 11, pp. 473–84

Johnson, C.E. and Petrie, T.A. (1995) 'The relationship of gender discrepancy to eating disorder attitudes and behaviors', *Sex Roles*, Vol. 33, pp. 405–16

Johnston, L., MacDonald, R., Mason, P., Ridley, L. and Webster, C. (2000) *Snakes and Ladders: Young People, Transitions and Social Exclusion*. Oxford: The Policy Press

Joiner, T.E., Schmidt, N.B. and Wonderlich, S.A. (1997) 'Global self esteem as contingent on body satisfaction among patients with bulimia nervosa: lack of diagnostic specificity?', *International Journal of Eating Disorders*, Vol. 21, pp. 67–76

Judge, T. (2001) 'A rose by any other name? Are self-esteem, generalised self-efficacy, neuroticism and locus of control indicators of a common construct?', in B.W. Roberts and R. Hogan (eds) *Personality Psychology in the Work Place*. Washington, DC: American Psychological Association

Kahne, J. (1996) 'The politics of self esteem', *American Educational Research Journal*, Vol. 33, pp. 3–22

Kaplan, H.B. (1980) 'Deviant behavior and self-enhancement in adolescence', *Journal of Youth and Adolescence*, Vol. 7, pp. 253–77

Kaplan, H.B., and Porkorny, A.D. (1976) 'Self-derogation and suicide: II. Suicidal responses, self-derogation and accidents', *Social Science and Medicine*, Vol. 10, pp. 119–21

Kaplan, H.B., Johnson, R.J. and Bailey, C.A. (1987) 'Deviant peers and deviant behavior: further elaboration of a model', *Social Psychology Quarterly*, Vol. 50, pp. 277–84

Kaplan, H.B., Martin, S.S. and Johnson, R.J. (1986) 'Self rejection and the explanation of deviance: specification of the structure among latent constructs', *American Journal of Sociology*, Vol. 92, pp. 384–411

Kaplan, H.B., Smith, P.B. and Pokorny, A.D. (1979) 'Psychosocial antecedents of unwed motherhood among indigent adolescents', *Journal of Youth and Adolescence*, Vol. 8, pp. 181–207

Kashubeck, S. and Christensen, S.A. (1995) 'Parental alcohol use, family relationship quality, self-esteem and depression in college students', *Journal of College Student Development*, Vol. 36, pp. 431–43

Katz, A. (2000) *Leading Lads*. London: Topman

Keddie, A.M. (1992) 'Psychosocial factors associated with teenage pregnancy in Jamaica', *Adolescence*, Vol. 27, pp. 873–90

Keefe, K. and Berndt, T.J. (1996) 'Relations of friendship quality to self-esteem in early adolescence', *Journal of Early Adolescence*, Vol. 16, pp. 110–29

Kelly, D.H. (1975) 'Tracking and its impact on self-esteem: a neglected dimension', *Education*, Vol. 96, pp. 2–9

Kendall, R.E. (1983) 'Alcohol and suicide', *Substance and Alcohol Actions/Misuse*, Vol. 4, pp. 121–7

Kendall-Tackett, K.A., Williams, L.M. and Finkelhor, D. (1993) 'Impact of sexual abuse on children: a review and synthesis of recent empirical studies', *Psychological Bulletin*, Vol. 113, pp. 164–80

Kendler, K.S., Gardner, C.O. and Prescott, C.A. (1998) 'A population-based twin study of self esteem and gender', *Psychological Medicine*, Vol. 28, pp. 1403–9

Kenny, D. (1994) *Interpersonal Perception: A Social Relations Analysis*. New York: Guilford

Kernis, M.H. (1993) 'The roles of stability and level of self-esteem in psychological functioning', in R.F. Baumeister (ed.) *Self-esteem: The Puzzle of Low Self-regard*. New York: Plenum

Kernis, M.H., Grannemann, B.D. and Barclay, L.C. (1989) 'Stability and level of self esteem as predictors of anger arousal and hostility', *Journal of Personality and Social Psychology*, Vol. 56, pp. 1013–23

Kienhorst, C.W., de Wilde, E.J., van den Bout, J., Diekstra R.F. *et al.* (1990) 'Characteristics of suicide attempters in a population-based sample of Dutch adolescents', *British Journal of Psychiatry*, Vol. 156, pp. 243–8

Kingsbury, S., Hawton, K., Steinhardt, K. and James, A. (1999) 'Do adolescents who take overdoses have specific psychological characteristics? A comparative study with psychiatric and community controls', *Journal of the American Academy of Child and Adolescent Psychiatry*, Vol. 38, pp. 1125–31

Kinnier, R.T., Metha, A.T., Okey, J.L. and Keim, J. (1994) 'Adolescent substance abuse and psychological health', *Journal of Alcohol and Drug Education*, Vol. 40, pp. 51–6

Kitano, H. (1989) 'Alcohol and drug use and self-esteem: a socio-cultural perspective', in A.M. Mecca, N. Smelser and J. Vasconcellos (eds) *The Social Importance of Self Esteem*. Berkeley, CA: University of California Press

Kjelsberg, E., Neegaard, E. and Dahl, A.A. (1994) 'Suicide in adolescent psychiatric inpatients: incidence and predictive factors', *Acta Psychiatrica Scandinavica*, Vol. 89, pp. 235–41

Kling, K.C., Hyde, J.S., Sowers, C.J. and Buswell, B.N. (1999) 'Gender differences in self esteem: a meta-analysis', *Psychological Bulletin*, Vol. 125, pp. 470–500

Konovsky, M. and Wilsnack, S.C. (1982) 'Social drinking and self-esteem in married couples', *Journal of Studies on Alcohol*, Vol. 43, pp. 319–33

Koo-Loed, J.H., Costello, N., Light, K.C. and Girdler, S.S. (2000) 'Women with eating disorder tendencies display cardiovascular, neuroendocrine and psychosocial profiles', *Psychosomatic Medicine*, Vol. 62, pp. 539–48

Kostanski, M. and Gullone, E. (1998) 'Adolescent body image dissatisfaction: relationships with self-esteem, anxiety and depression controlling for body mass', *Journal of Child Psychology and Psychiatry and Allied Disciplines*, Vol. 39, pp. 255–62

Koval, J.J., Pederson, L.J., Mills, C.A., McGrady, G.A. and Carvajal, S.C. (2000) 'Models of the relationship of stress, depression and other psychosocial factors to smoking behavior: a comparison of students in Grades 6 and 8', *Preventive Medicine: An International Journal Devoted to Practice and Theory*, Vol. 30, pp. 463–77

Kreitman, N. (1977) *Parasuicide*. London: Wiley

Kusel, A.B. (1999) 'Primary prevention of eating disorders through media literacy training of girls', *Dissertation Abstracts International: Section B: The Sciences and Engineering*, Vol. 60, No. 4-B, October, p. 1859

Laflin, M.T., Moore-Hirschl, S., Weis, D.L. and Hayes, B.E. (1994) 'Use of the theory of reasoned action to predict drug and alcohol use', *International Journal of Addictions*, Vol. 29, pp. 927–40

Leaf, R.C., Krauss, D.H., Dantzig, S.A. and Alington, D.E. (1992) 'Educational equivalents of psychotherapy: positive and negative mental health benefits after group therapy exercises by college students', *Journal of Rational Emotive and Cognitive Behavior Therapy*, Vol. 10, pp. 189–206

Leary, M.R., Tambor, E.S., Terdal, S.K. and Downs, D.L. (1995) 'Self-esteem as an interpersonal monitor: the sociometer hypothesis', *Journal of Personality and Social Psychology*, Vol. 68, pp. 518–30

Le Bon, G. (1896) *The Crowd: A Study of the Popular Mind*. London: Unwin

Lee, G.R. and Shelan, C.L. (1989) 'Social relations and the self-esteem of older persons', *Research on Aging*, Vol. 11, pp. 427–42

Leung, F., Schwartzman, A. and Steiger, H. (1996) 'Testing a dual-process family model in understanding the development of eating pathology: a structural equation modelling analysis', *International Journal of Eating Disorders*, Vol. 20, pp. 367–75

Lewinsohn, P.M., Rohde, P. and Seeley, J.R. (1994) 'Psychosocial risk factors for future adolescent suicide attempts', *Journal of Consulting and Clinical Psychology*, Vol. 62, pp. 297–305

Lloyd, C. (1998) 'Risk factors for problem drug use: identifying vulnerable groups', *Drugs: Education, Prevention and Policy*, Vol. 5, pp. 217–32

Luker, K. (1975) *Taking Chances: Abortion and the Decision not to Contracept*. Berkeley, CA: University of California Press

Lundy, J.R. (1972) 'Some personality correlates of contraceptive use among unmarried female college students', *Journal of Psychology*, Vol. 80, pp. 9–14

Lynam, D.R., Milich, R., Zimmerman, R., Novak, S.P., Logan, T.K., Martin, C., Leukefeld, C. and Clayton, R. (2000) 'Project DARE: no effects at 10-year follow-up', *Journal of Consulting and Clinical Psychology*, Vol. 67, pp. 590–3

Maag, J.W., Irvin, D.M., Reid, R. and Vava, S.F. (1994) 'Prevalence and predictors of substance abuse: a comparison between adolescents with and without learning difficulties', *Journal of Learning Disabilities*, Vol. 27, pp. 223–34

McCarthy, J.D. and Hoge, D.R. (1984) 'The dynamics of self-esteem and delinquency', *American Journal of Sociology*, Vol. 90, pp. 396–410

Mccauley, G.T. (1995) 'The relationship of self esteem and locus of control to unintended pregnancy and childbearing among adolescent females', *Dissertation Abstracts International: Section B The Sciences and Engineering*, Vol. 55, No. 7-B, p. 2678

McCord, W., McCord, J. and Howard, A. (1961) 'Family correlates of aggression in non-delinquent male children', *Journal of Abnormal and Social Psychology*, Vol. 62, pp. 79–93

MacCorquodale, P. and DeLamater, J. (1978) 'Self-image and premarital sexuality', *Journal of Marriage and the Family*, Vol. 41, pp. 327–39

McCreary, D.R. and Sasse, D.K. (2000) 'An exploration of the drive for muscularity in adolescent boys and girls', *Journal of American College Health*, Vol. 48, pp. 297–304

McFadden, J. (1998) 'NECTAR: natural eating, control theory and results', *International Journal of Reality Therapy*, Vol. 18, pp. 46–7

McFarlin, D.B. and Blaskovich, J. (1981) 'Effects of self-esteem and performance feedback on future affective preferences and cognitive expectations', *Journal of Personality and Social Psychology*, Vol. 40, pp. 521–31

McFarlin, D.B., Baumeister, R.F. and Blaskovich, J. (1984) 'On knowing when to quit: task failure, self-esteem, advice and nonproductive persistence', *Journal of Personality*, Vol. 52, pp. 138–55

McGee, R. and Williams, S. (2000) 'Does low self-esteem predict health compromising behaviours among adolescents?', *Journal of Adolescence*, Vol. 23, pp. 569–82

McNair, L.D., Carter, J.A. and Williams, M.K. (1998) 'Self-esteem, gender and alcohol use: relationships with HIV risk perception and behaviors in college students', *Journal of Sex and Marital Therapy*, Vol. 24, pp. 29–36

McWhirter, B.T. (1997) 'Loneliness, learned resourcefulness and self-esteem in college students', *Journal of Counseling and Development*, Vol. 75, pp. 460–9

Madianos, M.G., Gefou-Madianou, D., Richardson, C. and Stefanis, C.N. (1995) 'Factors affecting illicit and licit drug use among adolescents and young adults in Greece', *Acta Psychiatrica Scandinavica*, Vol. 91, pp. 258–64

Maney, D.W. (1990) 'Predicting university students' use of alcoholic beverages', *Journal of College Student Development*, Vol. 31, pp. 23–32

Marcenko, M.O., Fishman, G. and Friedman, J. (1999) 'Reexamining adolescent suicidal ideation: a developmental perspective applied to a diverse population', *Journal of Youth and Adolescence*, Vol. 28, pp. 121–38

Marciano, P.L. and Kazdin, A.E. (1994) 'Self-esteem, depression, hopelessness and suicidal intent among psychiatrically disturbed inpatient children', *Journal of Clinical Child Psychology*, Vol. 23, pp. 151–60

Martin, J.I. and Knox, J. (1997) 'Self-esteem instability and its implications for HIV prevention among gay men', *Health and Social Work*, Vol. 22, pp. 264–73

Matz, P.E. (1999) 'Body image dissatisfaction, teasing and acceptance of appearance standards in overweight women', unpublished doctoral dissertation, New York University

Mead, G.H. (1934) *Mind, Self and Society*. Chicago: University of Chicago Press

Mecca, A.M., Smelser, N.J. and Vasconcellos, J. (eds) (1989) *The Social Importance of Self Esteem*. Berkeley, CA: University of California Press

Meijboom, A., Jansen, A., Kampman, M. and Schouten, E. (1999) 'An experimental test of the relationship between self esteem and concern about body shape and weight in restrained eaters', *International Journal of Eating Disorders*, Vol. 25, pp. 327–34

Melnick, B. and Hurley, J.R. (1969) 'Distinctive personality attributes of child-abusing mothers', *Journal of Consulting and Clinical Psychology*, Vol. 33, pp. 746–9

Mitchell, R. (1975) 'The incidence and nature of child abuse', *Developmental Medicine and Child Neurology*, Vol. 17, pp. 641–4

Mookherjee, H.N. (1986) 'Comparison of some personality characteristics of male problem drinkers in rural Tennessee', *Journal of Alcohol and Drug Education*, Vol. 31, pp. 23–8

Morrison, D.M. (1985) 'Adolescent contraceptive behavior: a review', *Psychological Bulletin*, Vol. 98, pp. 538–68

Mruk, C. (1999) *Self-esteem: Research Theory and Practice*, 2nd ed. London: Free Association Books

Muller, J., Hicks, R. and Winocur, S. (1993) 'The effects of employment and unemployment on psychological well-being in Australian clerical workers: gender differences', *Australian Journal of Psychology*, Vol. 45, pp. 103–8

Nasser, E.H. and Overholser, J.C. (1999) 'Assessing varying degrees of lethality in depressed adolescent suicide attempters', *Acta Psychiatrica Scandinavica*, Vol. 99, pp. 423–31

Neumark-Sztainer, D., Storey, M., French, S.A. and Resnick, M.D. (1997) 'Psychosocial correlates of health compromising behaviors among adolescents', *Health Education Research*, Vol. 12, pp. 37–52

Newcomb, M.D., Maddahian, E. and Bentler, P.M. (1986) 'Risk factors for drug use among adolescents: concurrent and longitudinal analyses', *American Journal of Public Health*, Vol. 76, pp. 525–31

Nezlek, J.B., Kowalski, R.M., Leary, M.R., Blevins, T. and Holgate, S. (1997) 'Personality moderators of reactions to interpersonal rejection: depression and trait self-esteem', *Personality and Social Psychology Bulletin*, Vol. 23, pp. 1235–44

Oates, R.K. and Forrest, D. (1985) 'Self esteem and early background of abusive mothers', *Child Abuse and Neglect*, Vol. 9, pp. 89–93

O'Dea, J. and Abraham, S. (1999) 'Onset of disordered eating attitudes and behaviors in early adolescence: interplay of pubertal status, gender, weight and age', *Adolescence*, Vol. 34, pp. 671–9

O'Dea, J. and Abraham, S. (2000) 'Improving the body image, eating attitudes and behaviours of young male and female adolescents: a new educational approach that focusses on self esteem', *International Journal of Eating Disorders*, Vol. 28, pp. 43–57

Olmstead, R.E., Guy, S.M., O'Mally, P.M. and Bentler, P.M. (1991) 'Longitudinal assessment of the relationship between self esteem, fatalism, loneliness and substance abuse', *Journal of Social Behavior and Personality*, Vol. 6, pp. 749–70

Overholser, J.C., Adams, D.M., Lehnert, K.L. and Brinkman, D.C. (1995) 'Self-esteem deficits and suicidal tendencies among adolescents', *Journal of the American Academy of Child and Adolescent Psychiatry*, Vol. 34, pp. 919–28

Palumbo, D.J. and Ferguson, J.L. (1995) 'Evaluating Gang Resistance Education and Training (GREAT): is the impact the same as that of Drug Abuse Resistance Education (DARE)?', *Evaluation Review*, Vol. 19, pp. 597–619

Pandina, R.J. and Schuele, J.A. (1983) 'Psychosocial correlates of alcohol and drug use of adolescent students and adolescents in treatment', *Journal of Studies on Alcohol*, Vol. 44, pp. 950–73

Parish, J.G. and Parish, T.S. (1991) 'Support systems functionality, self concepts and alcohol use', *College Student Journal*, Vol. 25, pp. 470–2

Pastore, D.R., Fisher, M. and Friedman, S.B. (1996) 'Abnormalities in weight status, eating attitudes and eating behaviors about urban high school students: correlations with self esteem and anxiety', *Journal of Adolescent Health*, Vol. 18, pp. 312–19

Pelham, B. (1993) 'On the highly positive thoughts of the highly depressed', in R.F. Baumeister (ed.) *Self-esteem: The Puzzle of Low Self-regard*. New York: Plenum

Pelham, B. and Swann, W. (1989) 'From self-conceptions to self-worth: on the sources and structure of global self-esteem', *Journal of Personality and Social Psychology*, Vol. 57, pp. 672–80

Penny, G.N. and Robinson, J.O. (1986) 'Psychological resources and cigarette smoking in adolescents', *British Journal of Psychology*, Vol. 77, pp. 351–7

Perlman, D. (1974) 'Self-esteem and sexual permissiveness', *Journal of Marriage and the Family*, Vol. 36, pp. 470–3

Petraitis, J., Flay, B.R., Miller, T.Q., Torpy, E.J. and Greiner, B. (1998) 'Illicit subtance use among adolescents: a matrix of predictors', *Substance Use and Abuse*, Vol. 33, pp. 2561–604

Petrie, K. and Brook, R. (1992) 'Sense of coherence, self-esteem, depression and hopelessness as correlates of reattempting suicide', *British Journal of Clinical Psychology*, Vol. 31, pp. 293–300

Petrie, K., Chamberlain, K. and Clarke, D. (1988) 'Psychological predictors of future suicidal behaviour in hospitalized suicide attempters', *British Journal of Clinical Psychology*, Vol. 27, pp. 247–57

Petty, R.E. and Wegener, D.T. (1998) 'Attitude change: multiple roles of persuasion variables', in D. Gilbert, S. Fiske and G. Lindzey (eds) *Handbook of Social Psychology*, Vol. 1, 4th edition. New York: McGraw-Hill

Phelps, L., Sapia, J., Nathansen, D. and Nelson, L. (2000) 'An empirically supported eating disorder prevention program', *Psychology in the Schools*, Vol. 37, pp. 443–52

Piers, P.V. (1969) *Manual for the Piers-Harris Children's Self Concept Scale*. Nashville, TN: Counselor Recording and Tests, Department of Mental Health

Pitts, C. and Waller, G. (1993) 'Self-denigratory beliefs following sexual abuse: association with the symptomatology of bulimic disorder', *International Journal of Eating Disorders*, Vol. 13, pp. 407–10

Plotnick, R.D. (1992) 'The effect of attitudes on teenage premarital pregnancy and its resolution', *American Sociological Review*, Vol. 57, pp. 800–11

Plotnick, R.D. and Butler, S.S. (1991) 'Attitudes and adolescent nonmarital childbearing: evidence from the National Longitudinal Study of Youth', *Journal of Adolescent Research*, Vol. 6, pp. 470–92

Pope, A., McHale, S. and Craighead, E. (1988) *Self-esteem Enhancement with Children and Adolescents*. New York: Pergamon

POPS International Foundation (1994) *POPS Catalogue*. Myrtle Beach, SC: POPS International Foundation

Prause, J. and Dooley, D. (1997) 'Effect of underemployment on school leavers' self-esteem', *Journal of Adolescence*, Vol. 20, pp. 243–60

Rabe, J.J. (1998) 'Body image disturbances in anorexia nervosa', *Psychatria Polska*, Vol. 32 (supplement), pp. 15–23

Ramsey, R.D. (1994) *501 Ways to Boost Your Child's Self Esteem*. Chicago: Contemporary Books

Rees, C.D. and Wilborn, B.L. (1983) 'Correlates of drug abuse in adolescents: a comparison of families of drug abusers with the families of non-abusers', *Journal of Youth and Adolescence*, Vol. 12, pp. 55–63

Reynolds, W.M. (1991) 'Psychometric characteristics of the Adult Suicide Ideation Questionnaire in college students', *Journal of Personality Assessment*, Vol. 56, pp. 289–307

Rhodes, N. and Wood, W. (1992) 'Self esteem and intelligence affect influenceability: the mediating role of message reception', *Psychological Bulletin*, Vol. 111, pp. 156–71

Richards, M.H., Gitelson, I.B., Petersen, A.C. and Hurtig, A.L. (1991) 'Adolescent personality in girls and boys: the role of mothers and fathers', *Psychology of Women Quarterly*, Vol. 15, pp. 65–81

Richardson, A.G. (1987) 'Differences in adolescents' self-esteem across cultures', *Psychological Reports*, Vol. 61, pp. 19–22

Rieckert, J. and Moeller, A.T. (2000) 'Rational-emotive behavior therapy in the treatment of adult victims of childhood sexual abuse', *Journal of Rational Emotive and Cognitive Behavior Therapy*, Vol. 18, pp. 87–102

Riggio, R.E., Throckmorton, B. and De Paola, S. (1990) 'Social skills and self esteem', *Personality and Individual Differences*, Vol. 11, pp. 799–804

Rittner, B. and Smyth, N.J. (1999) 'Time-limited cognitive-behavioral group interventions with suicidal adolescents', *Social Work with Groups*, Vol. 22, pp. 55–75

Rittner, B., Smyth, N.J. and Wodarski, J.S. (1995) 'Assessment and crisis strategies intervention with suicidal adolescents', *Crisis Intervention and Time Limited Treatment*, Vol. 2, pp. 71–84

Robbins, C., Kaplan, H.B. and Martin, S.S. (1985) 'Antecedents of pregnancy among unmarried adolescents', *Journal of Marriage and the Family*, Vol. 42, pp. 567–83

Roberts, R.E., Roberts, C.R. and Chen, R.Y. (1998) 'Suicidal thinking among adolescents with a history of attempted suicide', *Journal of the American Academy of Child and Adolescent Psychiatry*, Vol. 37, pp. 1294–300

Robinson, R.B. and Frank, D.I. (1994) 'The relation between self-esteem, sexual activity and pregnancy', *Adolescence*, Vol. 29, pp. 27–35

Robinson, W.P., Tayler, C.A. and Piolat, M. (1990) 'School attainment, self-esteem and identity: France and England', *European Journal of Social Psychology*, Vol. 20, pp. 387–403

Rosen, J.T. and Shipley, R.H. (1983) 'A stage analysis of self-initiated smoking reductions', *Addictive Behaviors*, Vol. 8, pp. 263–72

Rosenbaum, M.E. and de Charms, R. (1962) 'Self-esteem and overt expression of aggression', in N.F. Washburne (ed.) *Decisions, Values and Groups*, Vol. 2. New York: Pergamon

Rosenberg, F. and Rosenberg, M. (1978) 'Self-esteem and delinquency', *Journal of Youth and Adolescence*, Vol. 7, pp. 279–91

Rosenberg, M. (1965) *Society and the Adolescent Self-image*. Princeton, NJ: Princeton University Press

Rosenberg, M. (1979) *Conceiving the Self*. New York: Basic Books

Rosenberg, M. and Pearlin, L.I. (1978) 'Social class and self-esteem among children and adults', *American Journal of Sociology*, Vol. 84, pp. 53–77

Rosenthal, R. (1994) *Meta Analytic Procedures for Social Research*. Beverley Hills, CA: Sage

Ross, H. E. and Ivis, F. (1999) 'Binge eating and substance use among male and female adolescents', *International Journal of Eating Disorders*, Vol. 26, pp. 245–60

Rotheram-Borus, M.J., Rosario, M., Reid, H. and Koopman, C. (1995) 'Predicting patterns of sexual acts among homosexual and bisexual youths', *American Journal of Psychiatry*, Vol. 152, pp. 588–95

Rubin, M. and Hewstone, M. (1998) 'Social identity theory's self-esteem hypothesis: a review and some suggestions for clarification', *Review of Personality and Social Psychology*, Vol. 2, pp. 40–62

Sands, R., Triker J., Sherman, C., Armatas, C. *et al.* (1997) 'Disordered eating patterns, body image, self-esteem and physical activity in preadolescent school children', *International Journal of Eating Disorders*, Vol. 21, pp. 159–66

Sanftner, J.L. and Crowther, J.H. (1998) 'Variability in self-esteem, moods, shame and guilt in women who binge', *International Journal of Eating Disorders*, Vol. 23, pp. 391–7

Schaeffer, G.M., Schuckit, M.A. and Morrissey, E.R. (1976) 'Correlation between two measures of self esteem and drug use in a college sample', *Psychological Reports*, Vol. 39, pp. 915–19

Scheff, T.J., Retzinger, S.M. and Ryan M.T. (1989) 'Crime, violence and and self esteem: review and proposals', in A.M. Mecca, N.J. Smelser and J. Vasconcellos (eds) *The Social Impotance of Self Esteem*. Berkeley, CA: University of California Press

Scheier, L.M., Botvin, G.J., Griffin, K.W. and Diaz, T. (2000) 'Dynamic growth models of self esteem and adolescent alcohol use', *Journal of Early Adolescence*, Vol. 20, pp. 178–209

Schneiderman, L., Furman, W.M. and Weber, J. (1989) 'Self-esteem and chronic welfare dependency', in A.M. Mecca, N.J. Smelser and J. Vasconcellos (eds) *The Social Importance of Self Esteem*. Berkeley, CA: University of California Press

Schuetz, A. (1998) 'Coping with threats to self-esteem: the differing patterns of subjects with high versus low trait self-esteem in first person accounts', *European Journal of Personality*, Vol. 12, pp. 169–86

Schulenberg, J., O'Malley, P.M., Bachman, J.G. and Johnston, L.D. (2000) '"Spread your wings and fly": the course of well-being and substance use during the transition to young adulthood', in L.J. Crockett and R.K. Silbereisen (eds) *Negotiating Adolescence in Times of Social Change*. New York: Cambridge University Press

Seiden, R.H. and Gleiser, M. (1990) 'Sex differences in suicide among chemists', *Omega: Journal of Death and Dying*, Vol. 21, pp. 177–89

Sendbueher, J.M., Kincel, R.L., Nemeth, G. and Oertel, J. (1979) 'Dimensions of seriousness in attempted suicide: significance of the Mf scale in suicidal MMPI profiles', *Psychological Reports*, Vol. 44, pp. 343–61

Shackelford, T.K. (2001) 'Self-esteem in marriage', *Personality and Individual Differences*, Vol. 30, pp. 371–90

Shisslak, C.M., Crago, M. and Estes, L.S. (1995) 'The spectrum of eating disturbances', *International Journal of Eating Disorders*, Vol. 18, pp. 209–19

Shorkey, C.T. (1980) 'Sense of worth, self-esteem and anomia of child-abusing mothers and controls', *Journal of Clinical Psychology*, Vol. 36, pp. 817–20

Shorkey, C.T. and Armendariz, J. (1985) 'Personal worth, self-esteem, anomia, hostility and irrational thinking of abusing mothers: a multivariate approach', *Journal of Clinical Psychology*, Vol. 41, pp. 414–21

Silbereisen, R.K., Schoenpflug, U. and Albrecht, H.T. (1990) 'Smoking and drinking: prospective analyses in German and Polish adolescents', in K. Hurrelmann and F. Loesel (eds) *Health Hazards in Adolescence: Prevention and Intervention in Childhood and Adolescence*. Berlin: Walter de Gruyter

Simons, R.L. and Murphy, P.L. (1985) 'Sex differences in the causes of adolescent suicide ideation', *Journal of Youth and Adolescence*, Vol. 14, pp. 423–34

Singh, H. and Mustapha, N. (1994) 'Some factors associated with substance abuse among secondary school students in Trinidad and Tobago', *Journal of Drug Education*, Vol. 24, pp. 83–93

Skager, R. and Kerst, E. (1989) 'Alcohol and drug use and self esteem: a psychological perspective', in A.M. Mecca, N.J. Smelser and J. Vasconcellos (eds) *The Social Importance of Self Esteem*. Berkeley, CA: University of California Press

Skitka, L.J. and Frazier, M. (1995) 'Ameliorating the effects of parental divorce: do small group interventions work?', *Journal of Divorce and Remarriage*, Vol. 24, pp. 159–79

Smart, R.G. and Ogburn, A.C. (1994) 'Street youth in substance abuse treatment: characteristics and treatment compliance', *Adolescence*, Vol. 29, pp. 733–45

Smelser, N.J. (1989) 'Self-esteem and social problems: an introduction', in A.M. Mecca, N.J. Smelser and J. Vasconcellos (eds) *The Social Importance of Self Esteem*. Berkeley, CA: University of California Press.

Stacy, A.U., Newcomb, M.D. and Bentler, P.M. (1992) 'Interactive and higher order effects of social influences on drug use', *Journal of Health Social Behavior*, Vol. 33, pp. 226–41

Stanley, L. and Arora, T. (1998) 'Social exclusion among adolescent girls: their self-esteem and coping strategies', *Educational Psychology in Practice*, Vol. 14, pp. 94–100

Steffenhagen, L.A. and Steffenhagen, R.A. (1985) 'Self esteem and primary demographic characteristics of alcoholics in a rural state', *Journal of Alcohol and Drug Education*, Vol. 30, pp. 51–9

Stengel, B. (1978) 'Some observations on repressive values in drug treatment', *Journal of Drug Issues*, Vol. 8, pp. 63–73

Stoil, M.J., Hill, G.A., Jansen, M.A., Sambranao, S. and Winn, F.J. (2000) 'Benefits of community-based demonstration efforts: knowledge gained in substance abuse', *Journal of Community Psychology*, Vol. 28, pp. 375–89

Streetman, L.G. (1987) 'Contrasts in the self-esteem of unwed teenage mothers', *Adolescence*, Vol. 22, pp. 459–64

Sutton, S.R., Marsh, A. and Matheson, J. (1990) 'Microanalysis of smokers' beliefs about the consequences of quitting: results from a large population sample', *Journal of Applied Social Psychology*, Vol. 20, pp. 1847–62

Tajfel, H. (1978) *Differentiation between Social Groups: Studies in the Social Psychology of Intergroup Relations*. London: Academic Press

Tantleff-Dunn, S. and Thompson, J.K. (2000) 'Breast and chest size satisfaction: relation to overall body image and self-esteem', *Eating Disorders: The Journal of Treatment and Prevention*, Vol. 8, pp. 241–6

Taylor, S. and Brown, J.D. (1988) 'Illusion and well-being: a psychological perspective on mental health', *Psychological Bulletin*, Vol. 103, pp. 193–210

Tennen, H. and Afleck, G. (1993) 'The puzzles of self esteem: a clinical perspective', in R. Baumeister (ed.) *Self-esteem: The Puzzle of Low Self-regard*. New York: Plenum

Thompson, K. (1989) 'Effects of early alcohol use on adolescents' relations with peers and self-esteem: patterns over time', *Adolescence*, Vol. 24, pp. 837–49

Toch, H. (1993) *Violent Men: An Inquiry into the Psychology of Violence*. Washington, DC: American Psychological Association

Townsend, M.A., McCraken, H.E. and Wilton, K.M. (1988) 'Popularity and intimacy as determinants of psychological well-being in adolescent friendships', *Journal of Early Adolescence*, Vol. 8, pp. 421–36

Tucker, L.A. (1984) 'Psychological differences between adolescent smoking intenders and nonintenders', *Journal of Psychology*, Vol. 118, pp. 37–43

Twamley, E.W. and Davis, M.C. (1999) 'The socio-cultural model of eating disturbance in young women: the effects of personal attributes and family environment', *Journal of Social and Clinical Psychology*, Vol. 18, pp. 467–89

van Aken, M.A. and Asendorpf, J.B. (1997) 'Support by parents, classmates, friends and siblings in preadolescence: covariation and compensation across relationships', *Journal of Social and Personal Relationships*, Vol. 14, pp. 79–93

van der Ham, T., van Strein, D.C. and van Egneland, H. (1998) 'Personality characteristics predict outcome of eating disorders in adolescents: a 4-year prospective study', *European Child and Adolescent Psychiatry*, Vol. 7, pp. 79–84

van Gastel, A., Schotte, C. and Maes, M. (1997) 'The prediction of suicidal intent in depressed patients', *Acta Psychiatrica Scandinavica*, Vol. 96, pp. 254–9

Vaux, A. (1988) 'Social and emotional loneliness: the role of social and personal characteristics', *Personality and Social Psychology Bulletin*, Vol. 14, pp. 722–34

Vega, W.A., Zimmerman, R.S., Warheit, G.J., Apospori, E. *et al.* (1993) 'Risk factors for early adolescent drug use in four ethnic and racial groups', *American Journal of Public Health*, Vol. 83, pp. 185–9

Vella, M.L., Persic, S. and Lester, D. (1996) 'Does self-esteem predict suicidality after controls for depression?', *Psychological Reports*, Vol. 79, p. 1178

Vernon, M., Green, J.A. and Frothingham, T.E. (1983) 'Teenage pregnancy: A prospective study of self-esteem and other sociodemographic factors', *Pediatrics*, Vol. 72, pp. 632–5

Veron-Guidry, S., Williamson, D.A. and Netemeyer, R.G. (1997) 'Structural modelling analysis of body dysphoria and eating disorder symptoms in preadolescent girls', *Eating Disorder: The Journal of Treatment and Prevention*, Vol. 5, pp. 15–27

Voss, K., Markiewicz, D. and Doyle, A.B. (1999) 'Friendship, marriage and self-esteem', *Journal of Social and Personal Relationships*, Vol. 16, pp. 103–22

Waller, G. and Hartley, P. (1994) 'Perceived parental style and eating psychopathology', *European Eating Disorders Review*, Vol. 2, pp. 76–92

Waller, G., Ruddock, A. and Cureton, S. (1995) 'Cognitive correlates of reported sexual abuse in eating-disordered women', *Journal of Interpersonal Violence*, Vol. 10, pp. 176–87

Warren, R., McLellarn, R.W. and Ponzoha, C. (1988) 'Rational-emotive therapy vs general cognitive-behavior therapy in the treatment of low self-esteem and related emotional disturbances', *Cognitive Therapy and Research*, Vol. 12, pp. 21–37

Weisman, J. (1991) 'Though still a target of attack, self-esteem movement advances', *Education Week*, Vol. 10, pp. 1, 15, 17

Wells, E.L. and Rankin, J.H. (1983) 'Self-concept as a mediating factor in delinquency', *Social Psychology Quarterly*, Vol. 46, pp. 11–22

Welsh, W.M. and Stewart, A.J. (1995) 'Relationships between women and their parents: implications for mid-life well-being', *Psychology and Aging*, Vol. 10, pp. 181–90

Werner, E.E. and Smith, R. (1977) *Children of Kauai*. Honolulu: University of Hawaii Press

West, C.K., Fish, J.A. and Stevens, R.J. (1980) 'General self-concept, self-concept of academic ability and school achievement: implications for "causes" of self-concept', *American Journal of Education*, Vol. 24, pp. 194–213

West, P. and Sweeting, H. (1997) '"Lost souls" and "rebels": a challenge to the assumption that low self-esteem and unhealthy lifestyles are associated', *Health Education*, Vol. 5, pp. 161–7

Wiest, W.M. (1965) 'A quantitative extension of Heider's theory of cognitive balance applied to interpersonal perception and self-esteem', *Psychological Monographs*, Vol. 79, No. 607 (whole issue)

Wilhelm, P. (2000) 'Mitigating college women's self esteem regarding their physical appearance: an experiment in advertisement impact and media literacy', unpublished doctoral dissertation, University of Alabama

Willcox, M. and Sattler, D.N. (1996) 'The relationship between eating disorders and depression', *Journal of Social Psychology*, Vol. 136, pp. 269–71

Williams, G.J., Power, K.G., Millar, H.R., Freeman, C.P. *et al.* (1993) 'Comparison of eating disordered and other dietary/weight groups on measures of perceived control, assertiveness, self-esteem and self-directed hostility', *International Journal of Eating Disorders*, Vol. 14, pp. 27–31

Wills, T.A. (1994) 'Self-esteem and perceived control in adolescent substance use', *Psychology of Addictive Behaviors*, Vol. 8, pp. 223–34

Wiltfang, G.L. and Scarbecz, M. (1990) 'Social class and adolescents' self esteem: another look', *Social Psychology Quarterly*, Vol. 53, pp. 174–83

Winefield, H.R., Winefield, A.H. and Tiggemann, M. (1992) 'Social support and psychological well-being in young adults: the multi-dimensional support scale', *Journal of Personality Assessment*, Vol. 58, pp. 198–210

Winefield, H.R., Winefield, A.H., Tiggemann, M. and Goldney, R.D. (1989) 'Psychosocial concomitants of tobacco and alcohol use in young Australian adults', *British Journal of Addiction*, Vol. 84, pp. 1067–73

Wood, A., Waller, G. and Gowers, S. (1994) 'Predictors of eating psychopathology in adolescent girls', *Eating Disorders Review*, Vol. 2, pp. 6–14

Yang, B. and Clum, G.A. (1996) 'Effects of early negative life experiences on cognitive functioning and risk for suicide: a review', *Clinical Psychology Review*, Vol. 16, pp. 177–95

Yoder, K.A. (1999) 'Comparing suicide attempters, suicide ideators and nonsuicidal homeless and runaway adolescents', *Suicide and Life Threatening Behavior*, Vol. 29, pp. 25–36

Zieman, G.L. and Benson, G.P. (1983) 'Delinquency: the role of self-esteem and social values', *Journal of Youth and Adolescence*, Vol. 12, pp. 489–500

Zimmerman, M. Copeland, L., Shope, J. and Dielman, T. (1997) 'A longitudinal study of self-esteem: implications for adolescent development', *Journal of Youth and Adolescence*, Vol. 26, pp. 117–42

Appendix: Research into the possible consequences of low self-esteem

Crime and delinquency

Jensen (1973) found some relation between low self-esteem and delinquency, but the strength of the association varied with other characteristics of the sample studied. The association was clearest among black adolescents from advantaged social backgrounds. Zieman and Benson (1983), however, found no relation between self-esteem and delinquency in their sample. More recently, Neumark-Sztainer et al. (1997) have had access to evidence collected from 12,000 adolescents which included measures of both self-esteem and delinquency. The correlations found in this cross-sectional study indicated a moderate effect size.

A couple of other studies (Gold and Mann, 1972; Kelly, 1975) have tested the proposition that low self-esteem is the mediator of an effect of poor academic performance on delinquency. In neither case was any clear support found for such a mediating role.

The more informative research, however, has gone beyond looking for simple correlations and has asked whether these correlations are consistent with low self-esteem *causing* delinquency, directly or indirectly. It should be recalled from the earlier discussion that simple correlations can by themselves reflect a number of different possibilities, including the influence of a third variable, and the best available option to distinguish between the possibilities is longitudinal research.

Rosenberg and Rosenberg (1978) claimed to find an effect of self-esteem on delinquency in the data from the American 'Youth in Transition' study. This is a study of almost 1,500 adolescents, surveyed on three successive occasions. However, John Bynner and colleagues (Bynner et al., 1981) argued there were flaws in the methods used by the Rosenbergs to analyse these data. Using more rigorous techniques, they could find little evidence that self-esteem influences delinquency. Wells and Rankin

(1983) also reanalysed the Youth in Transition evidence, using different statistical techniques and including some appropriate controls for third variable effects, but came to the same conclusion as Bynner et al.

McCarthy and Hoge (1984) had a new opportunity to explore the influence of self-esteem on delinquency in a sample of almost 2,000 adolescents who were surveyed at age 13, 15 and 17. Their self-esteem measures included the Rosenberg scale and a shortened version of the Coopersmith SEI. They also assessed delinquency on five dimensions. The design of the study allowed them to examine the effects of self-esteem on delinquency reported two years later. One major weakness of cross-sectional designs in which self-esteem and delinquency are assessed at the same time point (as in the Neumark-Sztainer et al. study cited above) is that any self-reported delinquency predates current self-esteem. Consequently, any association found between the two is more reasonably interpreted as an influence of delinquency on self-esteem than the reverse.

McCarthy and Hoge found that, whichever measure of either self-esteem or delinquency they considered, and whether they looked at influences between 13 and 15 or between 15 and 17, the links from self-esteem to delinquency were uniformly very weak (not even a weak effect size). Moreover, about half the effects were positive, half were negative. In their view, the only reasonable conclusion was that low self-esteem has no coherent effect on delinquency. The one criticism that might be raised here is that two years was too long an interval and that self-esteem might have changed in this time.

Kaplan's efforts to test his own esteem enhancement explanation involved a survey of over 3,000 11 to 13 year olds (Kaplan, 1980) at yearly intervals for three years. This is potentially therefore an important source of evidence as to the relationship if any between self-esteem and delinquency. What he expected to find was that children who were not already involved in deviant activities and whose initial self-esteem was low were more likely to become involved subsequently. He did find this relationship but most clearly among middle-class children and among girls.

Kaplan's explanation also requires that self-esteem should rise as a result of involvement in deviant activities. This he did not find. Critics have pointed to several problems with his methods of testing his explanation. Among these was his analysis of links between self-esteem and each of 28 forms of deviance separately. This dramatically increases the likelihood of measurement error and, on the face of it, combining the 28 forms into a single scale would have seemed a better strategy.

Kaplan may have proceeded as he did to allow a clear distinction between those who had and had not adopted deviant behaviours. Yet anyone who has undertaken research in this area would find it puzzling that such a distinction could be made within a population of 11 to 13 year olds. Taking any one of the 28 deviant activities by itself, one might identify a reasonable number of children who have not engaged in this activity. But the number who have engaged in none of them will be vanishingly small. It is more realistic to describe this age group as more or less involved in delinquencies, that is, as lying at different points along a continuum from low to high involvement.

At all events, evidence from the other longitudinal studies (Bynner et al., 1981; McCarthy and Hoge, 1984) is mixed. In the first case, an impact of delinquency on subsequent self-esteem is evident, but both the nature and the direction of this impact depend on initial self-esteem and age. The impact is clearest for those with low initial self-esteem ('initial' here means when first tested, which was at age 16). In this group, prior delinquency has a negative effect at 16, a positive effect at 17, but a negative effect on self-esteem at 18. At no age is the effect particularly strong. The

sample examined by McCarthy and Hoge was 13, 15 and 17 at the three ages tested. The effects of prior delinquency on self-esteem were, at all three age levels, negative but small and progressively diminishing with age. In other words, delinquency seemed to have a small effect – it lowered self-esteem. The effect therefore was in the opposite direction to that predicted by Kaplan's argument.

Kaplan nonetheless performed further analyses on his own data to try and find his predicted effects (Kaplan et al., 1986, 1987). Confusingly, in the first of these, it was also predicted that low self-esteem would have both positive and negative effects on delinquency. However, low self-esteem was found to have a weak *negative* effect on subsequent deviance: low self-esteem resulted in less, not more deviance.

The second analysis introduced a new variable, deviant peer association. Interestingly, they found, as others have, that a delinquent inclination leads young people into associations with peers who are similarly inclined. Having friends who are delinquent does not turn one into a delinquent. Note that this is also inconsistent with the argument that adolescents with low self-esteem will become involved in delinquency because they are more vulnerable to peer group influence in this direction.

Finally, a more recent examination of the Kaplan esteem enhancement model by Jang and Thornberry (1998) failed to find any support for this model. Low self-esteem did not lead to delinquent behaviour. And engaging in delinquent behaviour did not raise self-esteem.

Drug use and drug abuse

A number of studies of the link between drug use or abuse and self-esteem go no further than attempting to determine whether an association exists at all. Among such studies, those by Finke and Williams (1999) on drug use by eight to 12 year olds, Howard and Jenson (1999) on inhalant use, Rees and Wilborn (1983) on drug abuse and

Carvajal *et al.* (1998) on substance abuse, each report an association with low self-esteem. So also do Cookson (1994); Ghindia and Kola (1996); Gordon and Caltabiano (1996); Gutierres and Reich (1988); and Kinnier *et al.* (1994).

Other studies have failed to find any association between self-esteem and drug use or abuse. These include Maag *et al.*'s (1994) study of marijuana use in a learning disabled sample and Biggs *et al.*'s (1983) study of solvent abuse. These conflicting findings may owe something to the small sample sizes in these studies, especially if the true association is not strong and if its strength varies with other factors such as age, gender, ethnicity or social background.

Larger samples should therefore provide clearer evidence but have not always done so. For example, Pandina and Schuele's (1983) survey of almost 2,000 12 to 28 year olds revealed an association between low self-esteem and substance use. However, their 'substance abuse' measure was a composite index which combined both alcohol and drug use, so in principle low self-esteem might have been related to one but not the other. The wide age range further obscures the picture.

A similarly wide age range – 14 to 28 years – was also a feature of Singh and Mustapha's (1994) study of 1,600 Trinidadians. Low self-esteem 'appeared', as the authors noted in their report, to be a factor in drug use but other factors emerged as more clearly implicated in this study. Vega *et al.*'s (1993) survey of 6,760 12 to 13 year old males in America identified low self-esteem as one of ten risk factors for 'illicit drug' use.

A couple of the other studies based on larger samples have failed to find any association at all. Thus, Laflin *et al.* (1994) found no link between low self-esteem and drug use among 2,000+ American high school and college students. Similarly, Hays *et al.* (1986) found no relation in a sample of 1,100 13 to 28 year olds, after controlling for possible confounding influences.

The much larger sample – over 12,000 11 to 21 year olds – Neumark-Sztainer *et al.* (1997) were able to study included measures of substance abuse. In this case, they found a link with low self-esteem, but the association was very modest (a correlation of 0.2). One way of illustrating the consequence of such a correlation is to note that, if everyone in the sample had the same level of self-esteem, the variations in drug use would be reduced by 4 per cent.

Other researchers have reported associations between low self-esteem and various kinds of drug use (e.g. Bry, 1983; Dishion *et al.*, 1988; Madianos *et al.*, 1995; Wills, 1994). But a recurring theme in their reports is that low self-esteem is but one among several risk factors, and often one of the less important. Wills, for example, notes that a variable he labelled 'perceived control' explains more than six times as much of the variance in substance use as is explained by self-esteem.

A few studies have looked at the possibility that self-esteem mediates the effects of other variables on drug use. These include the investigation by Dembo *et al.* (1987) which revealed that, for a sample of juvenile inmates, experience of physical abuse appeared to result in drug use and that this was partly mediated by the effect of such abuse on self-esteem. Andrews and Duncan (1997) found, in a longitudinal study, that low academic motivation at 13 led to later marijuana use and that this effect was partly mediated by the impact of academic motivation on self-esteem.

More generally, there is a dearth of good evidence for causal links of this kind. Such evidence would require longitudinal studies and most of the studies to date have simply surveyed a sample of young people on one occasion. Thus, the full range of possible explanations for any observed association between self-esteem and drug use could apply. In particular, low self-esteem could be a result rather than a cause of drug abuse, a result for example of loss of self-control associated with addiction. Given concurrent assessment of self-esteem and drug use, the latter is actually temporally prior to the former (a problem earlier encountered with respect to studies of delinquency and self-esteem). Low self-esteem and problem drug use could also be two effects that have a common cause, for example, physical abuse by parents or carers. This is known to be a risk factor for later drug misuse (Lloyd, 1998) and to be a negative influence on later self-esteem (as discussed in Chapter 3).

An interesting study by Smart and Ogburn (1994) compared young people living on the street and others. They found that the street youth were more depressed, had lower self-esteem, and had higher use of alcohol and drugs. It is possible that their lower self-esteem has led to their drug use but it is equally possible that these two things share a common cause, such as family conflict.

One recently published study that is in a better position to sort out causes draws on a longitudinal study in New Zealand. The authors of this study, McGee and Williams (2000), could find no influence of earlier self-esteem on later cannabis use. Petraitis *et al.* (1998) reviewed a number of prospective studies of drug abuse. Some of these had included self-esteem as a potential predictor but low self-esteem did not emerge as a significant risk factor in any of them.

A ten-year longitudinal study, spanning the period from late adolescence to early adulthood and based on a sample of 1,227 young people (Olmstead *et al.*, 1991), came to a different conclusion. Olmstead and his colleagues found that self-esteem in adolescence did predict substance abuse in adulthood. But the stronger predictor was substance abuse in adolescence. Ideally, this study would have included assessment of other risk factors for substance abuse known to be related to self-esteem such as parental neglect and abuse. In their absence, it is not possible to decide whether low self-esteem plays a mediating role in adult substance abuse, whether it has a direct and independent effect, or whether it has no role, being merely a correlated outcome.

Finally, if low self-esteem leads to drug abuse, then it should in theory be possible to reduce drug use by raising self-esteem. Hopkins *et al.* (1988) were able to find no carry-over effect of an educational programme to instil self-esteem upon subsequent drug use. Likewise, Stoil *et al.* (2000) report that activities that raise self-esteem have no consistent effect on substance use.

Smoking

A correspondence between low self-esteem and smoking among adolescents has been reported by various researchers. Penny and Robinson (1986), for example, found that smokers among a sample of almost 300 13 to 15 year olds had lower self-esteem than their peers who did not smoke. Conrad and colleagues (1992), reviewing evidence from a number of studies, noted that broad indicators of self-esteem emerged from these as related to smoking. But the relation was not very strong or clear, and not as substantial as that regularly reported between smoking and various other psychological and social attributes. Fidler *et al.* (1992) found that smoking was associated with lower levels of self-esteem in a sample of young people – aged 12 to 25 – with special educational needs and in a sample of controls. A similar finding was reported by Ahlgren *et al.* (1982) for a sample of some 600 12 to 12 year olds.

It is difficult to know what to make of these findings given these were not prospective studies. The usual possibilities still remain to be ruled out, notably that status as a smoker affects self-esteem or that both this status and current self-esteem are products of other conditions. There are, moreover, as many negative results in the literature as positive. West and Sweeting (1997) found no relation between self-esteem and smoking in their sample of Scottish youngsters. The results of studies by Goddard (1990) and by Jackson *et al.* (1998) were almost equally negative.

The evidence reported by McGee and Williams (2000) carries particular weight here as it does come from a prospective study. Earlier self-esteem did not predict later smoking. A German/Polish study (Silbereisen *et al.*, 1990) had a further advantage of looking at potential influences over a short period, a one-year interval. There were weak effects of self-esteem on nicotine consumption one year later, but only among the younger Germans surveyed (over the period from 14 to 15) and the older Poles (the period from 15 to 16). Most recently, Koval and his colleagues (2000), in a study of 1,543 teenagers, found that self-esteem at age 12 did not predict smoking two years later.

One study, by Stacy *et al.* (1992), has considered a different possibility, namely that self-esteem moderates the impact of peer influence on adolescent decisions to smoke. In a sample of 1,245 high school students, they did find that various psychological characteristics moderated this impact, but self-esteem was not one of them.

Other researchers have explored the potential role of self-esteem with respect to intentions, either intentions of non-smokers to start or of current smokers to quit. With respect to the first, Botvin *et al.* (1992) found that low self-esteem predicted intention to start smoking in a sample of 600 or so 13 to 14 year olds. However, Tucker (1984) had earlier found that level of self-esteem did not distinguish between 15 year olds intending to take up smoking and those who did not share this intention. At the same time, several other psychological variables did distinguish these two groups.

With respect to intention to quit, Sutton *et al.* (1990) found that smokers from 16 upwards expected higher self-esteem to be a gain from quitting. According to findings reported by Rosen and Shipley (1983), however, self-esteem did not predict intention to quit. Interestingly it did predict actual smoking reduction. Those with high self-esteem were more successful in achieving short-term reductions.

Alcohol abuse

The familiar difficulties of untangling cause and effect are equally applicable here. Several studies have compared the self-esteem of diagnosed alcoholics with that of non-alcoholics. The findings have been very consistent: the alcoholics have lower self-esteem (e.g. Carroll *et al.*, 1982; Ghadirian, 1979; Gross and Adler, 1970; Hendin, 1974; Kendall, 1983; Mookherjee, 1986; Stengel, 1978). Moreover, there are indications that female alcoholics have even lower self-esteem than male alcoholics (Beckman, 1978).

This very consistent pattern for alcoholics is also consistent with the view that low self-esteem is the consequence of alcoholism rather than a cause. Or, rather, it is a consequence of the public identity involved. For example, when people join Alcoholics Anonymous, they must agree to label themselves in extremely negative terms, as having reached a state of 'pitiful and incomprehensible demoralisation', as 'powerless over alcohol', as 'hitting bottom' and so on.

In their review of this literature, Skager and Kerst (1989) explicitly acknowledge this possibility:

> It can always be argued that people who have experienced the humiliation, shame and guilt usually associated with addiction, who have been labeled as alcoholics or addicts, or who find themselves in a chemical dependency treatment program suffer from low self-esteem because of their addiction.
> (p. 260)

But people do not just 'find themselves' in treatment programmes for addictions. They are placed there by courts, directed there by medical advice, or make the choice themselves. In one way or another, there is a public statement of extreme personal failure. This is consistent with another finding, that high alcohol users with low self-esteem are more likely to seek treatment (Charalampous *et al.*, 1976).

Moreover, a greater impact of alcoholism on female self-esteem would be consistent with the more mixed cultural messages about *male* inebriation. The cultural standards for female conduct tend to be clearer in this area. Konovsky and Wilsnack (1982) found that the self-esteem scores of women, but not men, went down after drinking alcohol. Moreover, the impact on self-esteem was strongest among those women who were most committed to a traditional view of the female role. In one of the few longitudinal studies in this area, Thompson (1989) found that regular alcohol consumption early in adolescence actually seemed to boost self-esteem later in adolescence, but only among those who equated drinking with sophistication.

Research with groups who have not yet been negatively labelled is more likely to tell us whether low self-esteem leads to alcohol abuse. A few studies of college students have reported a link between heavy alcohol use and low self-esteem. This was true, for example, of the findings reported by Schaeffer *et al.* (1976). Maney (1990) found that higher alcohol consumption was associated with lower self-esteem but was also more common among male than among female students. In contrast, Parish and Parish (1991) found an association between self-esteem and motives for drinking rather than how much alcohol was consumed. College students in this study with lower self-esteem were more likely to drink to gain peer acceptance.

This last finding is consistent with the conclusions from a large-scale study of adolescents that peer pressure is the main determinant of adolescent alcohol use (Dielman *et al.*, 1989). This same study, of 4,000+ adolescents, suggests no particular causal role for self-esteem. However, the findings reported by Dielman and his colleagues are open to other and, I suspect, more plausible interpretations. Young people who like to drink a lot hang out with each other. Those who are less enthusiastic about consuming a lot of alcohol prefer to associate with peers who share their views. If this is so, the origin of these contrasting preferences still has to be explained.

To date, there is little to support differences in self-esteem as the source of these inclinations. West and Sweeting found no association between levels of alcohol consumption and self-esteem in their survey of Scottish teenagers. The negative evidence from prospective studies is even more compelling. Winefield *et al.* (1989) surveyed a group of Australians at age 19 and again at 22. Level of self-esteem at the earlier time did not predict subsequent levels of alcohol use. Likewise, the evidence from the longitudinal study in New Zealand reported by McGee and Williams revealed no association between earlier self-esteem and later alcohol use. This was also the conclusion to which Newcomb *et al.* (1986) came on the basis of an eight-year longitudinal study, as did Silbereisen *et al.* (1990) looking at influences over one-year intervals. Finally, Scheier *et al.* (2000), in a longitudinal study of 740 adolescents, found that increases in alcohol consumption were more likely among those who had higher self-esteem at the outset.

Sexual behaviour and teenage pregnancy

Drummond and Hansford (1991) found that, as they put it, 'some' of the pregnant teenagers they interviewed had low self-esteem. Keddie's (1992) conclusion from a study of Jamaican teenagers is clearer. The self-esteem of non-pregnant adolescents was higher than that of their once-pregnant counterparts. Plotnick (1992) found in a survey of 1,142 adolescents that pre-marital pregnancy was associated with lower self-esteem. Werner and Smith (1977) found the same association.

Others have failed to find this association. Barth *et al.* (1983), comparing teenage mothers, pregnant teenagers and non-pregnant teenagers, did not find that the first two groups were particularly distressed compared to the last. Likewise, both Brunswick (1971) and Streetman (1987) found no difference in the self-esteem of teenagers who had and had not been pregnant. And Robinson and Frank (1994), as noted earlier, found no statistically significant relation between self-esteem and pregnancy.

This last study reveals two problems, however. First, the incidence of pregnancy in a representative sample is quite low. This affects the probability of detecting a statistically significant association even if such an association actually exists in the population from which one has sampled (risking the 'Type II' error referred to earlier). In the Robinson and Frank sample, the incidence was around 10 per cent.

The second problem is the age range sampled. If this is large – Robinson and Frank's sample ranged from 13 to 29 – it includes people for whom pregnancy can have highly positive connotations as well as those among whom pregnancy would carry a social stigma. For these reasons, large samples and the opportunity to look at narrow age bands provide more useful evidence.

Prospective studies have generally been based on larger samples and have produced somewhat clearer results. Kaplan and colleagues (1979) found that, of a sample of 14- to 15-year-old girls, those who had become mothers had low self-esteem scores a little over a year earlier. Robbins *et al.* (1985) returned to this sample when they were 21 and found that lower self-esteem at age 13 to 14 was associated with greater risk of pregnancy before 21, but the association was quite weak.

More recently, Plotnick and Butler (1991) published results from a study of 1,184 girls surveyed at age 14 and again at 19. By age 19, 17 per cent had given birth out of wedlock and this group had lower self-esteem scores at 14. A smaller-scale longitudinal study by Herrenkohl and colleagues (1998) indicated that teenage parenthood (i.e. before 20) was associated with lower self-esteem in childhood, as evaluated by teachers. Interestingly, teenage parenthood was also associated with childhood experience of physical abuse and neglect, suggesting a possible mediating role of self-esteem.

In contrast, Vernon *et al.* (1983) found no association between level of self-esteem and subsequent likelihood of teenage pregnancy. There are various reasons why no association showed up in this study. The negative results could be due to the particular self-esteem measure used (the Coopersmith scale) or to the age of the sample; for example, Crockenberg and Soby (1989) point out that many of the females in this sample, being somewhat older than those in other studies, would already have been sexually active when first surveyed. This could have had an esteem-enhancing effect. Whether or not this particular criticism has merit, this study is the exception.

An analysis by Mccauley (1995) of data from the American National Longitudinal Youth Survey is potentially the most informative so far published. The sample is large; almost 3,000 girls were surveyed. The survey was repeated at yearly intervals, which allowed estimates of the likelihood of pregnancy each year. Mccauley examined the likelihood at ages 16, 17, 18 and 19 and found that it was a little over one-and-a-half times higher for teenagers with lower self-esteem scores in the previous year.

If we are to conclude, as seems reasonable, that low self-esteem in adolescence carries a moderately increased risk of subsequent pregnancy as a teenager, what is the reason for this risk? Do teenagers with low self-esteem become sexually active at an earlier age, have more frequent sexual relations, or take less effective precautions against pregnancy? Each of these should increase the risk.

Looking first at sexual intercourse, low self-esteem does not seem to give rise to earlier or more frequent intercourse. Once again, the meaning of evidence from cross-sectional studies is ambiguous but the picture provided by such studies is quite consistent. Teenagers' sexual activity is either unrelated to their self-esteem or it is associated with *higher* self-esteem. Among the studies in which no association was found are those by Cvetkovich and Grote (1980) and by West and Sweeting (1997).

McGee and Williams (2000) did find an association between low self-esteem and early sexual activity, but this association disappeared once the correlated effects of family background were taken into account. In contrast, Jessor and Jessor (1975) found a *positive* association between self-esteem and loss of virginity. Furthermore, as this was also a longitudinal study, they were able to show that higher self-esteem preceded loss of virginity. However, they only found this association clearly among the males in their sample.

A study by Herrold and Goodwin (1979) points in a similar direction for females but less decisively. They found that females with lower self-esteem were more likely to approve of abstinence. Those with higher self-esteem described themselves as more willing to take the sexual initiative and less prone to guilt about their sexual behaviour.

An earlier study of college students (Perlman, 1974) indicates the importance of cultural norms and young people's attitudes to these norms. Perlman found that higher self-esteem was positively related to number of sexual partners, though only among those with a more liberal view of the norms. The fact that Herrold and Goodwin failed to find this association may reflect a change in those norms and attitudes towards them as awareness of the risks of sexually transmitted disease, and particularly HIV infection, increased.

Among the more recent studies, sampling a potentially more AIDS-aware generation, Neumark-Sztainer *et al.* (1997) found no association between self-esteem and unsafe sexual activities. Hollar and Snizek (1996), however, found high self-esteem was associated with more risky practice with respect to conventional sexual behaviour. They found precisely the reverse association – high self-esteem predicted safer practice – with respect

to unconventional behaviours, those characteristic of homosexual relations.

These apparently contradictory results may reflect a growing belief, at least among the kind of college-educated population from which they sampled, that the real health risks lie in unconventional sexual behaviours involved in gay sex. Consistent with this, Rotheram-Borus *et al.* (1995) report that higher self-esteem was associated with less risk taking among gay and bisexual males. Martin and Knox (1997) found something very similar. In a sample of 455 gay and bisexual men, unprotected intercourse with non-primary partners was more likely among those with lower self-esteem.

The most significant direct risk factor for pregnancy, as for sexually transmitted disease, is the adequacy and appropriateness of contraceptive practice. Oral contraceptives reduce the first risk, condom use reduces both. Several studies have indicated that adolescents with higher self-esteem are more likely to take appropriate precautions (e.g. Ager *et al.*, 1982; Cvetkovich and Grote, 1980; Herrold *et al.*, 1979; Hornick *et al.*, 1979; McNair *et al.*, 1998). But the picture is still mixed. In one of the studies, the association was found only among males and, in another one, it was found only among females.

Other studies fail to find any association. This is true of Lundy's (1972) study, although he expected the association to be negative because, at the time, pre-marital sex was more strongly disapproved of. Garris *et al.* (1976) and McCorquodale and DeLamater (1978) also both failed to find any link. A review by Morrison (1985) of adolescent contraceptive behaviour concluded that variables like self-esteem played, if any role at all in such behaviour, only a very minor role.

Child abuse

Several studies have reported an association between child abuse and low self-esteem. These include Culp *et al.*'s (1989) study of physically abusive mothers, Anderson and Lauderdale's (1982) study of abusive parents, Hamilton *et al.*'s (1987) study of abusive parents, Oates and Forrest's (1985) study of abusive mothers, as well as those by Melnick and Hurley (1969), Evans (1980) and Green *et al.* (1974). Two exceptions have both come from the same reseacher. Shorkey (1980) found no difference in the self-esteem of a sample of abusing mothers and controls, and reported the same result with a further study five years later (Shorkey and Armendariz, 1985).

In a sense, Shorkey's results are the more surprising. Parents who are labelled as child abusers attract considerable public revulsion, as newspaper coverage of such cases clearly shows. In the face of uniformly hostile public reaction, once a parent has been identified as an abuser, it might be very difficult for that parent to continue describing themselves in highly positive terms. The same issue arises with respect to convicted child molesters, who also turn out to have lower self-esteem than comparison groups (Fisher *et al.*, 1999).

An uncontaminated estimate of the effects of parents' self-esteem on the treatment of their children could only be provided by a prospective study in which self-esteem is assessed before any abuse comes to light. But studies of this kind are more costly for various reasons. Among these are the need for a large sample. Whatever the true prevalence rate for child abuse – and charities like Childline claim it is far higher than the detection rate – the numbers actually detected are small. Abusers who have remained undetected may not be especially willing to own up to researchers, even in confidence. Thus, one needs a rather large initial sample if it is to include enough identified abusers later on to compare statistically with the others.

These reasons may explain the paucity of longitudinal prospective studies. I have been able to identify only one to date. Christensen *et al.* (1994) found that mothers eventually identified as abusers did not differ at all from the other mothers in the survey in self-esteem as initially measured. The problem even with this study is that the group of 'non-abusers' may well include undiscovered abusers, so masking any difference between true abusers and true non-abusers.

Economic consequences

One difficulty here is that there are still few adequately designed studies but Caputo's (1998) is potentially one of them. He used the data from the US National Longitudinal Study of Youth. Its design allows one to look for effects of self-esteem on outcomes later in life. Caputo could find no discernible pattern of influence of self-esteem on subsequent economic well-being. Economically marginalised youth did not become more marginalised as a result of low self-esteem.

Interestingly, Dooley and Prause (1997) came to a different conclusion looking at the same data. They found that self-esteem in adolescence was related to employment status seven years later. They interpreted this as indicating that high self-esteem is a psychological asset that aids those who have it to secure and hold on to employment. The disparity in conclusions drawn from the same evidence underlines the importance of controlling for correlated variables. Had this latter analysis included control for the effect of educational attainment – the personal asset that really matters here, and correlated slightly with self-esteem – it is possible that the apparent effect of self-esteem would have disappeared. But maybe not.

Feinstein's (2000) analysis of data from the British Cohort Study (BCS) does clearly indicate an impact of low self-esteem on certain economic outcomes, even after controlling for the effects of educational qualifications, but the pattern is quite complex. The BCS has three great advantages for our purposes. First, because it is a prospective study, clearer conclusions can be drawn about the causal priority of self-esteem (measured in this study when the participants were aged ten).

Second, information is available from a large and representative sample. Third, a large number of other variables were measured in the study and so it is possible to exclude several effects that might otherwise be confounded with those of low self-esteem.

The economic outcomes considered by Feinstein are experience of unemployment by age 26 and earnings at this age. Age ten self-esteem does not predict experience of short spells of unemployment (less than four months consecutively), but it does predict longer periods of unemployment. The patterns for males and females, however, are quite different. Among the former, those with lower self-esteem at age ten were the more likely to have been unemployed for long periods by age 26. Among females, the differences were only between those with very high and very low self-esteem, but in the opposite direction; those with very *high* self-esteem were more likely to have experienced long periods of unemployment.

It is possible to construct stories for each of these results. For males, one might propose that initial experiences of unemployment are more damaging to those with lower self-esteem, leaving them with insufficient confidence to successfully pursue opportunities for re-employment. For females, perhaps exceptionally high self-esteem leads to rejection of re-employment opportunities seen as incommensurate with their own high assessment of their worth. But any explanation will remain speculative and ad hoc in the absence of further evidence.

There are similar ambiguities about the effects of self-esteem on earnings. As Feinstein's analyses show, there clearly are such effects though self-esteem only plays a significant role here for males. In their case, the scale of the effect is similar to that of key intellectual abilities measured at ten. In other words, it is quite substantial. As to why self-esteem has this result, it may be that people with higher self-esteem push harder for a good income or are less tolerant of low pay. An alternative is

Brockner's (1988) argument: employees with high self-esteem are perceived by their supervisors to be more productive workers, using time more effectively and requiring less guidance.

But, if self-esteem as such has any of these consequences, how could it thereby affect the earnings of males but not females? Given the quality of the evidence on which they are based, Feinstein's results cannot easily be discounted. They point to important long-term consequences of childhood self-esteem.

Eating disorders

First of all, a simple association between low self-esteem and indices of eating problems, whether the indices satisfy strict diagnostic criteria for anorexia or bulimia or more relaxed criteria, looks to be incontrovertible. The studies by Willcox and Sattler (1996), Coric and Murstein (1993) and Koo-Loed *et al.* (2000) all found an association between bulimia and low self-esteem. Rabe (1998) found an association for anorexics compared to controls. Williams *et al.* (1993) found that diagnosed anorexics and bulimics both had lower self-esteem than controls. Johnson and Petrie (1995) found that anorexic and bulimic symptoms among college girls were associated with lower self-esteem.

The picture is similar for other indicators of disordered eating. Shisslak *et al.* (1995), reviewing the literature on binge eating, identified low self-esteem as one of its correlates and, more recently, Matz (1999) has reported a direct connection between low self-esteem and binge eating among young women, as have Ross and Ivis (1999) in a sample of 1,000 teenage girls. Abrams *et al.* (1993) have found an association between low self-esteem and indicators of disordered eating, as have O'Dea and Abraham (1999) and Ghaderi and Scott (1999), these last in a sample of 1,157 females aged 18 to 20. Ghaderi and Scott also report a prevalence rate for eating disorder in this group of 8 per cent. Neumark-Sztainer and colleagues (1997) found, in their survey of 12,000 adolescents, that low self-esteem was related to unhealthy weight loss, though the association was not strong (correlations in the range 0.1 to 0.2). Hubbard et al. (1998) found that food-related exercisers had lower self-esteem than people who exercised for other reasons. The motive for the exercise thus appears to be important. Evidence reported by Iannos and Tiggeman (1997) indicates that self-esteem is not related to excessive exercise per se.

Self-esteem also appears to be connected to attitudes towards eating. Several studies have employed a standard scale to measure these attitudes, the EAT (Eating Attitudes Test), which has been shown to be predictive of disordered eating habits. Studies finding this connection include those by Canals et al. (1996); Fisher et al. (1994); Pastore et al. (1996); and Pitts and Waller (1993). The first of these, however, found self-esteem to be unrelated to *frequency* of binge eating.

The general picture, then, is one in which eating disorders of all kinds are associated, though not necessarily very strongly, with low self-esteem. This would seem inconsistent with the two interpretations outlined above, each of which anticipates that self-esteem will be associated with some disorders but not others. Nonetheless, the associations could exist for different reasons with respect to different forms of eating disorder. In this context, Sanftner and Crowther (1998) found that the self-esteem of binge-eating female students varied more than that of non-binge eaters. They also found, however, that self-esteem was higher rather than lower prior to binge-eating episodes, suggesting consolation is not the motive.

There are also indications that eating disorders are linked to self-esteem in the sense that Rosenberg defined it, namely as general feelings about the self rather than as the sum of a set of evaluations of the self. Grubb et al. (1993) found that the Coopersmith evaluative measure was not related to indicators of eating disorders, as did Griffiths et al. (1999). The latter found that a relation

emerged only when self-esteem as assessed by the Rosenberg affective scale was considered. Moreover, this was true irrespective of the type of eating disorder.

Still, the discovery of an empirical association leaves much of the work to be done. In this particular case there is the obvious possibility that the disorder has an effect on self-esteem. So, for example, the lack of self-control involved in binge eating may leave a person feeling disgusted with themselves. Alternatively, the admission of an eating disorder of any kind may be humiliating perhaps because it attracts disapproval, contempt or pity from others. It is less easy, however, to see how eating *attitudes* could adversely affect self-esteem.

Inevitably, prospective studies provide stronger grounds for claims about a causal sequence here. The prospective studies so far published all find that low self-esteem predicts later indications of eating disorder, though with varying degrees of certainty. Among these, the New Zealand evidence reported by McGee and Williams (2000) shows that lower self-esteem in childhood predicted eating disorders in adolesence. Button et al. (1996), in a study of approximately 600 girls, found that self-esteem level at 11 to 12 years predicted risk of developing more severe symptoms of eating disorder at 15 to 16. However, Wood et al. (1994) found that the self-esteem of a sample of adolescent girls predicted eating attitudes (EAT scores) two years later, but not eating disorders. And Calam and Waller (1998) reported that self-esteem at 12 years was only weakly related to indications of eating disorder seven years later.

The authors of this last study make a further important observation, indicating that prospective studies will not necessarily provide unequivocal answers to causal questions. They note that characteristic patterns of eating are quite consistent across time. The better predictors of 19 year olds' eating problems were eating attitudes at age 12. Ideally, a prospective study allows one to determine whether a quality like self-esteem predicts change in the outcome of interest ('change' here can include the later appearance of a behaviour that was not previously present, as well as, for example, change in the severity or frequency of this behaviour). To achieve this, the investigators will need to include assessment of the presence or level of the outcome of interest at the start of the study as well as at the end.

A good example of this is the four-year prospective study conducted by van der Ham *et al.* (1998). They found that the initial level of self-esteem predicted whether bulimics were better or worse by the end of the four years. In effect, they did not expect or find that low self-esteem *causes* bulimia but did find that low self-esteem affects the course of the disorder, making recovery more difficult. Hesse-Biber *et al.* (1999) similarly found that eating-disordered women with lower self-esteem were less likely to recover.

A different kind of causal evidence is potentially available from studies of intervention programmes designed either to reduce the risk of eating disorder or to help recovery. A couple of recent reports evaluate programmes focusing on self-esteem (O'Dea and Abraham, 2000; Phelps *et al.*, 2000). In each case, the programme succeeded on both counts; self-esteem went up and eating disorder symptoms went down. It is tempting to conclude that the effects on symptoms were due to the changes in self-esteem, but this would be premature. A stronger case for this conclusion would be present if the degree of amelioration of symptoms was directly and strongly related to the degree of increase in self-esteem. Otherwise, it remains possible that the programme has resulted in other changes that are responsible for the impact on symptoms or that both self-esteem and the symptoms themselves have been directly but independently affected by participation in the programme. Unfortunately, however, even a strong association between the extent of these two kinds of change would not tell us which caused which.

Showing in addition that self-esteem changed first would be more decisive.

Nonetheless, the programme described by O'Dea and Abraham does contain some clues about the roots of eating disorders. Their programme attempted to uncouple self-esteem from perceptions of appearance. And in this it was apparently successful. By the end of the programme, appearance mattered less to the participants. This bears on the reasons for the large observed sex differences in vulnerability to eating disorders.

One obvious question is why females are so many times – perhaps ten times – more likely to develop eating disorders of any kind than males. The difference is far too large to be accounted for by any general tendency for women to have lower self-esteem than men. One popular explanation is that women's self-esteem is much more closely linked to their physical appearance than it is for men. Women are more preoccupied with an ideal body shape and appearance, and with the extent to which their own bodies match this ideal. Their sense of their own worth is in turn more closely bound up with the degree to which a match is present. One would further have to assume either that the ideal is unrealistic or that some women misjudge their own degree of discrepancy from the ideal.

This suggests a causal pathway from body dissatisfaction to self-esteem and from self-esteem to eating disorder. The associations implied by this pathway have certainly been observed. Ideal body size is related to self-esteem (Sands *et al.*, 1997). Eating disorders are associated with body dissatisfaction (e.g. Leung *et al.*, 1996; Twamley and Davis, 1999) and self-esteem is related to body weight dissatisfaction among females (e.g. Beamer, 1999; Meijboom *et al.*, 1999) but, according to one study, not among males (Furnham and Calman, 1998). The self-esteem of males, however, may be linked to dissatisfaction with other aspects of their bodies, notably chest size and musculature (cf.

Tantleff-Dunn and Thompson, 2000). Thus, McCreary and Sasse (2000) found that low self-esteem was related to a drive for muscularity among 16- to 24-year-old males.

Support for the mediating role of self-esteem in the relation between body dissatisfaction and disordered eating is more mixed, however. Leung *et al.* (1996) claimed to find support for this mediating role in their study of around 900 adolescent girls. The observation by Joiner *et al.* (1997) of a stronger relation between body dissatisfaction and self-esteem among bulimic adolescents than among non-disordered adolescents also points to such a role. In contrast, Twamley and Davis (1999) interpret their own findings, derived from 249 female college students, as confirming that self-esteem is one of a number of factors *moderating* the impact of body dissatisfaction on eating behaviour. They are saying, in other words, that self-esteem is not itself influenced by body dissatisfaction but low self-esteem does magnify the effect of dissatisfaction on eating. A further possibility, endorsed by Darnall *et al.* (1999) on the basis of their study of Brazilian adolescents, is that low self-esteem is both an independent factor, not a mediator, and a direct influence on level of preoccupation with weight. Thus, they see weight concern as mediating the impact of self-esteem on eating pathology rather than the other way around.

Several other proposals have been made for a mediating role of self-esteem. These include the proposal that experience of sexual abuse increases the risk of subsequently developing an eating disorder because the abuse experience damages self-esteem (Waller *et al.*, 1995). This is consistent with the evidence reported by Hernandez (1995) from a survey of over 6,000 adolescents. She found that indications of eating disorder were correlated with both reports of earlier physical and sexual abuse and low self-esteem.

Frederick and Grow (1996) propose that feelings of lack of autonomy reduce self-esteem and this in turn increases the risk of eating disorder. For Fryer and colleagues (1997), self-esteem mediates the impact of stressful experiences on disturbed eating. Another suggestion (Waller and Hartley, 1994) is that parental disapproval directly lowers self-esteem and indirectly, as a result of this, leads to eating problems.

Whether these are plausible explanations – each needs further research at this stage – they would also need to show why these causal sequences are more likely to be found among females. Another difficulty is that mediation requires a quite strong relation between the mediator and the outcome. If the remote cause – experience of sexual abuse or other stressful experiences, parental disapproval or lack of autonomy – works through the mediator, it will only have an effect on the outcome to the extent that it has an impact on the mediator. The mediator – self-esteem – should therefore be more strongly linked to both the remote cause and the outcome than either are to each other. The difficulty is that correlations observed between self-esteem and eating disorders have not generally been strong.

Suicide, suicide attempts and suicidal thoughts

Numerous studies indicate a simple association between low self-esteem and suicide ideation in a variety of age and cultural groups (e.g. De Man *et al.*, 1992, 1993; Gonzalez *et al.*, 1998; Marciano and Kazdin, 1994; Reynolds, 1991; Sendbuehler *et al.*, 1979; van Gastel *et al.*, 1997; Vella *et al.*, 1996). One interesting exception is the investigation by Beer and Beer (1992). Scores on the Coopersmith index were unrelated to suicide ideation, suggesting, as with eating disorders, that the association is with feelings about the self rather than with a set of evaluations of the self.

Others also find an association between low self-esteem and parasuicide (e.g. Boudewyn and Liem, 1995; Overholser *et al.*, 1995; Petrie *et al.*, 1988;

also reviews by Rittner *et al.*, 1995; Yang and Clum, 1996). However, Nasser and Overholser (1999) found no relation of self-esteem to the lethality of the attempts.

A rather smaller number of longitudinal studies also find that self-esteem predicts later suidical ideation. These include McGee and Williams's (2000) analysis of their New Zealand data and an investigation by Goldney *et al.* (1991) of adolescents' levels of self-esteem on extent of suicidal thinking eight years later. Kaplan and Pokorny (1976) found that, among 4,694 American high school pupils, a self-derogation measure was related to number of accidents reported one year later. They interpreted accidents as potential suicide attempts or at least failures to take proper care of oneself.

A small number of longitudinal studies have considered self-esteem as a predictor of later suicide attempts, though, in all cases, in combination with other risk factors. Considered on its own, self-esteem does predict subsequent suicide attempts (e.g. Lewinsohn *et al.*, 1994). Kjelsberg *et al.* (1994) followed up 1,800 adolescents who had been psychiatric patients and found that about 2 per cent had committed suicide over that period. Those who did so had lower self-esteem than the average for the group at the time they were first studied. An examination by Seiden and Gleiser (1990) of chemists who had committed suicide indicated that they had lower than average self-esteem, though it is not entirely clear how this was determined retrospectively.

How can we determine whether self-esteem is not only a risk factor for suicide-related outcomes but also an important one? The first step is to recognise the many other risk factors and assess these simultaneously. Major risk factors for suicide include living alone, lack of social support, drug use, physical illness, depression, knowing others who have made suicide attempts or completed them, a history of prior attempts, experience of victimisation and economic difficulties. These may

also be the risk factors for parasuicide and suicidal ideation. Consequently, research into the causes of suicide-related outcomes should ideally assess the full range.

Many studies have assessed the impact of a range of factors. However, in examining these, one is struck by two things. The first is that, in several cases, no attempt is then made to decide on the relative importance of each factor. This is vital because some factors may be correlated with the outcome only because they are also associated with one of the other factors. So, for example, self-esteem may relate to suicide attempts only because it is also related to social isolation or victimisation. And it may be related to these either because it is a causal factor – for instance, it influences the likelihood of vicitimisation which in turn is the direct cause of suicide attempts. Or it may be a correlated outcome – social isolation may depress self-esteem *and* lead to suicide attempts.

The second observation is that, when the appropriate statistical analyses are performed, whether or not self-esteem emerges as a predictor, and how significant a predictor it turns out to be, depend very largely on what other factors were included in the analysis. There are, however, consistent features of those studies in which self-esteem drops out of contention once other risk factors are considered.

Studies in which self-esteem survived as a predictor after taking into account the effects of other predictors include Kjelsberg *et al.*'s (1994) 15-year follow-up of adolescents who had been psychiatric inpatients. Self-esteem was one among a set of eight factors discriminating the suicides from the still living. Garnefski *et al.* (1992) found, in a study of Dutch 15 to 16 year olds, that suicidal thoughts and behaviours were related to low self-esteem but also and independently to use of drugs, experience of sexual abuse and feelings of loneliness. Another Dutch survey, but on a much larger scale (Kienhorst *et al.*, 1990) – a sample of 9,393 14 to 20 year olds – revealed a range of risk factors independently predicting suicide attempts, including self-esteem but also family breakdown and alcohol and drug use among them. Hershberger *et al.* (1997) looked at predictors of suicide attempts among lesbian, gay and bisexual youth. They found that the attempters had lower self-esteem but had also suffered more adverse consequences – loss of friends, victimisation, and so on – as a result of revealing their sexual orientation.

A distinguishing feature of studies in which self-esteem does not survive as a predictor or in which its significance at best is greatly reduced is that they included other measures of affect or feelings about the self. Petrie and Brook (1992) found that extent of suicidal ideation among parasuicides was best predicted by a variable which they called 'sense of coherence' and which seemed to reflect the degree to which their participants felt their lives were meaningful. Previous history of suicide attempts, unemployment and living alone enhanced prediction.

Beautrais *et al.* (1999) found that a sample of suicide attempters under 25 were distinguished by higher neuroticism (which is also sometimes identified as 'negative affect'), hopelessness, introversion, an external locus of control and low self-esteem. But low self-esteem ceased to be a significant predictor when the other factors were taken into account. In Kingsbury *et al.*'s (1999) study of overdosers, self-esteem was a correlate but its effect disappeared once level of depression was taken into account. The outcome of Marcenko *et al.*'s (1999) analysis of predictors of suicidal ideation was very similar. Roberts *et al.* (1998) examined predictors of suicidal ideation, including self-esteem, in a large (5,000+) sample of ten to 17 year olds. The surviving predictors were history of suicide attempts, depression and recent life stresses. Simons and Murphy (1985) found that self-esteem was correlated with occurrence of suicidal behaviour in a sample of high school students but not when other factors were considered. Emotional problems and involvement in delinquency were predictors for females; employment problems were most potent predictors for males. Finally, De Man (1999) looked directly at the consequences for the association between self-esteem and suicidal ideation of taking into account the effects of depression. The consequence was to reduce substantially the strength of this association.

In some other studies including measures of affective variables in addition to self-esteem, the latter does survive as a predictor though typically not as the most important one. This is true, for example, in the Lewinsohn *et al.* (1994) study. Of the 1,500 14 to 28 year olds surveyed, 26 made suicide attempts one year into the study. Low self-esteem at entry predicted these attempts, but so did history of past attempts, suicidal ideation and depression. Similarly, in Yoder's (1999) study of homeless youth and runaways, five factors distinguished those reporting suicidal ideation from those not doing so. The factors were self-esteem, depression, experience of physical abuse, experience of sexual abuse and having a friend who attempted suicide.

What all this suggests is that measures going by different names are to some extent assessing the same thing. Measures of depression, negative affect (or neuroticism), self-esteem, hopelessness, fatalism, and locus of control are all attempting to assess a person's feelings about themselves. Depending on how each measure is constructed, the overlap may be almost complete or it will be more partial. It is a fair bet that an aspect of these feelings is implicated in suicidal thoughts and actions. But, whichever measure does the best job of assessing this particular aspect will emerge from the analysis as the predictor and others which measure it less well will fall away.